"As long as I have been in media and communications, it never ceases to amaze me how many folks, especially in the Church, know little or nothing about how to tap into — well, media and communications. Even though we're called by Jesus Himself to go out into the whole world and preach the Good News, often despite the countless opportunities in today's vast media landscape, the Good News doesn't get much further from the front door and barely makes it onto the parish web site. That's why Donna A. Heckler's book, *Marketing God*, is so badly needed. We are, after all, the Lord's hands and feet, and *Marketing God* can help any ministry, diocese, or individual take some major marketing steps in the right direction."

— **TERESA TOMEO**, media expert, motivational speaker, best-selling author, syndicated Catholic talk show host of Catholic Connection and The Catholic View for Women

"In her book *Marketing God*, author Donna A. Heckler draws upon her many years as a successful corporate brand marketer to show the reader how proven techniques utilized in a business environment can also be effective in building up a parish or any faith-based organization. Her helpful examples and observations on how successful brand development and management can be applied to evangelization efforts make this a must-read for anyone involved in the work of the Church."

— **ALAN NAPLETON**, president of the Catholic Marketing Network

"Donna A. Heckler provides those ministering in the Church real insight to how we, as Church, can build relationships that reveal God's everyday presence. Her approach of providing a lot of ideas in a simple-to-follow format challenges the reader to take some simple steps in 'marketing God.'"

— **FR. ED PRATT**, Pastor at Church of the Ascension, Kettering, Ohio

"How do we get the Catholic message across in this secular age? In her book *Marketing God: Inspired Strategies for Building the Kingdom*, Donna A. Heckler suggests we 'fight fire with fire.' In other words, adopt strategies that have spelled success in the corporate world of marketing. We all buy into their genius — how many daily choices have been made for us by brand name advertisers? Now the author, who spent years successfully promoting well-known brands, lays out a detailed plan applying the best the world has to offer to promote the Good News."

— **Sr. Mary Lea Hill, FSP**, writer, editor, and author of
Prayer and You: Wit and Wisdom from a Crabby Mystic and
Blessed are the Stressed: Secrets to a Happy Heart from the Crabby Mystic

"Donna masterfully correlates Bible verses to marketing strategies and demonstrates how the Bible and faith can guide each of us as we share our ministries, parishes, and organizations with others. All we need to do is ask: Matthew 7:7–8."

— **Pamela Evans**, founder and president of
Evans Consulting Group, Cleveland, Ohio

"As a former Corporate Executive and a recent revert to the Faith, I used to say, 'The Catholic Faith needs a new marketing plan!' Lo and behold, Donna A. Heckler has done just that! Her easy to read, easy to understand principles rooted in faith will help anyone in a ministry to further expand God's Kingdom here on earth. Long overdue, thank you, Donna."

— **Kendra Von Esh**, Catholic author and speaker,
and TV news anchor Shalom World

MARKETING
GOD

MARKETING GOD

Inspired Strategies for
Building the Kingdom

Donna A. Heckler

Our Sunday Visitor
Huntington, Indiana

Our Sunday Visitor Publishing Division

Our Sunday Visitor, Inc.
200 Noll Plaza
Huntington, IN 46750
www.osv.com
1-800-348-2440

ISBN: 978-1-68192-400-7 (Inventory No. T2294)
eISBN: 978-1-68192-401-4
LCCN: 2019936311

Cover design: Tyler Ottinger
Cover art: Shutterstock
Interior design: Amanda Falk

PRINTED IN THE UNITED STATES OF AMERICA

This book is dedicated to Saint Paul,
who was truly one of the most
effective marketers of God.

CONTENTS

FOREWORD

Building and marketing strong brands plays a very important role in our economy — it helps consumers find a good match between the needs that they have and the myriad of products and services competing for attention.

These consumer needs can be as basic as protection from the weather (Patagonia clothing) or unexpected life events (Farmers Insurance). These needs can be at a more abstract level, such as the need for enjoyment (Norwegian Cruise Line) or to express our values (Volvo cars). Irrespective of the wide spectrum of needs that we have (even a need for spiritual fulfillment) and the myriad of brands populating (some might say cluttering) the marketplace, marketing is the basic process of communicating a meaningful proposition about a brand that will tap into a basic human need.

Donna A. Heckler brings a wealth of marketing and brand building experience across a variety of industries along with her own deep faith commitment to exploring how marketing and brand building principles can benefit spiritually based enterprises.

This book introduces many fundamental principles that have been time-tested — principles such as the importance of focus, brand clarity, empathy with the customer, simplicity, and consistency. Donna demonstrates through example how these principles help faith-based organizations better connect with their constituencies and help to make a stronger statement of the organization's principles and values.

The short chapters you will find here weave together, in a very accessible way, contemporary branding concepts with examples of how these concepts have been successfully applied in practice. This book will hold up well over time and serve as a valuable resource over the years.

Brian D. Till
James H. Keyes Dean of Business Administration and
Professor of Marketing at Marquette University, coauthor
of *The Truth About Creating Brands People Love*

AUTHOR'S PREFACE

The premise of this book is very simple. I explore how we can take the elements that cause people around the world to become loyal to a brand and use these techniques to help people find God again.

I have spent my career in marketing. My expertise is in creating brands that matter, that are relevant, that are motivating to people. In today's society, we measure success by gain, and according to that standard I know I succeeded as a marketing professional. Brands I have worked on have sold hundreds of millions — in fact, billions — of dollars globally. You probably know some of those brands: Energizer, Trane, Enterprise, Kimball, Red Cross, the list goes on.

Marketing is very much about human behavior. Why do people do what they do? How can we understand people so that we can guide them to purchase our product, our service, our brand? The end goal is to make people highly loyal to your brand. When they are loyal, they will always use the brand. Moreover, they will suggest your brand to friends and make others loyal to it as well.

As a deeply committed Catholic, I have long wondered what could happen in our Church if we applied the science of marketing to faith, to God. Would the strategies work? Could those in ministry and pastoral positions use the tools that succeed in marketing to build God's kingdom? Could these strategies help us in our work of saving souls?

I venture to say yes.

About ten years ago, I coauthored a successful book, *The Truth About Creating Brands People Love*. The book included fifty-one pithy little topics about building brands. In this new book, I take a similar approach. In fact, I pull several of the insights that were most relevant and most effective, and I use them here as part of the framework for how we can talk about marketing God.

For many people of faith, especially those who are pastors or involved in leading ministries, the concept of "marketing God" is troubling at best, or blasphemous at worst. The reality, of course, is that it can be problematic. God is not a product. This book does not speak of marketing God as an end in itself, but as a means to the all-important end of bringing people to God and being loyal to him. I have had the privilege to know and work alongside many men and women who have a deep love of God. Their joy swells from the depth of their souls, and their hearts yearn to share that joy with others. Yet too often they lack the knowledge of how to draw people to faith-based events, let alone to faith. They need tools to get people in the door. That's where the strategies we use in marketing come in.

That's why I wrote this book. I hope it provides those sharing the Good News with tools that are relevant in today's world. I hope that through this book, those of us focused on sharing faith can help more people become loyal to God.

Introduction

GOD'S PORTFOLIO
OF BRANDS

G od is big — really big — infinite, in fact. That means we cannot contain God, we cannot hold him in our hand, and we cannot even begin to understand his complexity. Granted, we have guides such as the Bible, the Church, and theologians, but we can never comprehend God. So when we want to "market" our relationship and our insights to draw people to God, what should we do?

Secular brands that we know are usually rooted in tangible items or services that are easy to understand. A battery, for example, fits in the palm of my hand. I know how it works, and I know what it does. It really is quite simple. A Trane air conditioner, while quite a bit bigger, is still pretty easy to grasp. I can see its size and come to understand its complexity. Even when dealing with brands who provide services, not products, I have a sense of what I'm getting. I understand what H&R Block does, for instance: they provide tax preparation services.

Big companies with multiple brands, various products, and a variety of target audiences use what is called a "portfolio strategy" for marketing. When we are considering faith from a marketing perspective, I suggest we look to a portfolio model for insights. In portfolio marketing, the idea is that different products will meet different needs for consumers. One brand does not have to be everything to everyone. In fact, that is a sure recipe for failure. An easy example comes from farming. If you wanted to plant corn seeds one year, you would purchase the brand DeKalb. If you were interested in planting soybeans the next year, you would purchase Asgrow. The same farmer makes the purchases, and he does so from the same company, Bayer's Crop Science division, but he is able to make his purchases according to his specific needs each year by choosing different brands in Bayer's portfolio.

We can apply this model when we think about sharing God. When we have a mission or apostolate that shares God, we have to keep in mind that we are part of the whole. There is no one person in our Church who can share everything. Some are very good at sharing and reflecting on Scriptures; others may have a deep understanding of building faith; others may have insights into the role of women in a faith community. People need these understandings at different times in their lives. Your role in your parish, ministry, or apostolate is to be part of this enormous portfolio, all committed to leading people to God when your specialty, gift, or service is needed in their lives.

We cannot answer every little item with our work, or with our messaging. That's okay. Remember, when we speak of "marketing God," the one calling all the shots is God. He is the one who sees it all, who understands it all. He knows what the world needs, and you have answered his call, which is why you are here. Our work is to market and communicate our part of God's brand portfolio as effectively as possible.

Let this book serve as your guide.

Truth 1

THE HARDEST PART IS DONE

*"All things were made through him, and
without him was not anything made that
was made. In him was life, and the life was the
light of men. The light shines in the darkness,
and the darkness has not overcome it."*
— JOHN 1:3–5

The hardest part of marketing is creating demand. It is hard to get people to understand that they want or even need your brand, your product, or your service, so the best marketers are skilled at creating demand.

Honestly, does anyone really have to have $250 Nike shoes? No. But Nike has done a marvelous job of creating demand. They have inspired people to "Just Do It" with the not-so-subtle message that you can do it better if you are wearing Nike shoes. Nike has invested much of their marketing activity in the creation of demand, getting people to desire their shoes.

Creating demand is expensive. When you are creating demand, you are often creating a new category, defining a new service, offering a new concept. That requires significant research to understand your customers and significant investment in educating them on why your solution answers the need they didn't even know they had.

The good news for those of us seeking to use marketing strategies to build God's kingdom is that we do not have to create demand. People inherently seek God. How do we know this? First of all, as Christians we know that we were made in God's likeness, and God is love. God has placed the desire for love within each of us. Moreover, we see people throughout the world seeking love, seeking purpose. The psychologist Abraham Maslow was one of the early psychologists to identify this foundational need. He famously outlined a hierarchy of needs, which prioritizes human requirements in a pyramid model. In this model, love and belonging are listed among those needs that must be satisfied to achieve self-actualization. More recently, social researcher Hugh Mackay, in his book *What Makes Us Tick*, posits that two of the top ten desires of humans include "something to believe in" and "love." People seek love by nature, and this means they are seeking God, even though they may not call him out by name.

The point is that people deeply desire God, even if they think they don't. In marketing vernacular, the "demand" already exists. That means that the first critical step is already completed.

That does not mean the task is easy. Many people have a difficult time recognizing that what they want most deeply is God. Your first challenge is an education challenge: to help people understand that your ministry, your service, your apostolate can help them to find what they seek. You do not have to invest in creating demand, but in drawing lines of sight between the longing people have for God and the service or ministry that you provide.

Saint Teresa of Calcutta is a beautiful example of recognizing the true demand. She understood that people are longing for love. Her ministry of helping the poor, especially the dying, was in direct response to this demand. Yet there was another demand, one that was less apparent. People needed to be shown their own deep desire to work alongside her in serving those in need. Not only did she invest in providing services to the poor, but she also invested in educating communities about people's dire needs and how to meet them.

As you consider your ministry and efforts, think about what demand you are addressing. What is the real need you are seeking to fill? How are you answering this need? Once you understand this, you can spend your energy, time, and money showing people how what you have to offer fills that need. The demand is there, and you are called to answer it.

FOR REFLECTION

As you look around you, what needs do you personally feel called to meet?

In today's materialistic society, what are some ways you can help people realize their true need for God?

Truth 2

BRAND AND MARKETING ARE NOT BAD WORDS

"Let no evil talk come out of your mouths, but only such as is good for edifying, as fits the occasion, that it may impart grace to those who hear."
— EPHESIANS 4:29

O ften, those who work in religious organizations and functions feel the need to avoid words like *brand* or *marketing* in anything they say or do. The word *communication* is always fine, but *brand* and *marketing* are considered bad and are to be avoided at all costs.

Unfortunately, the secular world has pounced on those words, suggesting that everything is a brand, and everything is marketed. Of course, in the secular world, the result of effective branding and marketing is money, money, and more money. In other words, *brand* and *marketing* are equated with *greed* and *commerce*. No wonder faith-based institutions shy away from using those words.

Yet, when we lose the words, we also lose the robust understanding that accompanies them. When the veneer of commercialization is removed, *brand* and *marketing* have deep meanings that can make a great difference for those who work in faith-based institutions, if they understand them appropriately.

A brand actually packs a very valuable punch. It is a way of encompassing everything the world sees and hears about a particular product, service, or organization. At its simplest level, a brand is a promise being made to a customer. That promise is conveyed in a variety of ways, and each item is part of the brand. A brand often includes a logo, a trademark, a tagline, colors and fonts, experiences, the products or services provided, key messages, etc. Every last piece that connects with a customer is housed under the title of brand. Objectively, that concept of a brand is not a bad thing.

Where the word *brand* runs into trouble is when the secular world equates brands with big business. Yet this equation misses a critical piece: a strong brand leads to loyalty, commitment, and trust. In the business world, loyalty and trust lead to sales, which contribute to the growth of businesses. For faith-based entities, however, loyalty, trust, and commitment lead to something far more important than money: they lead to deepening of faith, relationship with God, and service to others. The brand — the promise — of faith-based organizations is profound, and it is not commercial.

Think about EWTN as a brand. Many Catholics the world over know it; they recognize the logo, the letters, the name. Most importantly, they understand that it is a source for outstanding Catholic content. People are exceptionally loyal to EWTN, and for many it is the only source of the day's news. EWTN understood very well that the creation of a brand was about developing loyalty with a committed viewing audience. The result has been an ability to provide outstanding faith-based insights worldwide.

If *brand* equates to the promise or the *what* that you do, *marketing* describes how you get the word, the promise out there. Again, the secular world clouds the word *marketing* with the idea of really big budgets, aggressive media, and inappropriate creativity. At its core, however, marketing is communicating your brand or your message to appropriate audiences. Secular companies ratchet up their approaches, and their brash voices cause faith-based entities to draw away, fearful of the assertive attitude marketing seems to demand.

This is not what marketing has to be. Marketing can and should be a tool for ministries, parishes, and organizations that allows them to share their faith-based work with others.

Reflecting on the example of EWTN, they do have an enormous marketing advantage in that they are a media company; therefore, they are able to use their outlets to market themselves. You find them in social media, in print, radio, and, of course, TV. They have the message, a brand that matters to people, and they have the vehicles, the marketing ability to effectively reach their audience.

I am not suggesting that you should adopt these secular words in your everyday language for your ministry. However, I do hope that by understanding them, you will not be afraid of them. In this book, these words are used consistently, in large part because they are precise descriptors of important efforts. Both of the words *brand* and *marketing* are steeped in meaning, and when understood they can help you connect even more deeply with those you are trying to reach. I invite you to reflect on them, that they may impart grace as you strive to bring your message to life.

For Reflection

*What is your perception of the words **brand** and **marketing**?*

How can you use the principles of branding and marketing to better connect with others and draw them closer to God?

Truth 3

NOBODY WILL LOVE YOUR BRAND THE WAY YOU LOVE IT

"Thy words were found, and I ate them,
and thy words became to me a joy
and the delight of my heart."
— JEREMIAH 15:16

What you do every day often reveals your passions. If you run a religious organization, lead the communications for a ministry, or serve as pastor of a parish, chances are you are passionate about your work. You live and breathe life into it, ensuring work is done, bills are paid, and the organization's efforts are communicated.

Yet, no matter how much you love your organization — your brand — no one else will love it like that. They can't. They are happy simply to remember it on occasion.

The truth is, people are busy, and they are bombarded every day with things that need their attention. Think about this fun fact: a study done in 2005 by Yankelovich Inc. showed that the average person saw more than five thousand marketing messages a day,[1] and this did not include everything we encounter now on the internet and social media. Now more than ever, your brand is simply one of many things vying for people's attention.

When you think, hope, and act as if everyone loves your brand the way you do, you run into challenges. People get to your brand at different times in their lives, for different reasons. In particular, faith-based brands seek to awaken a deeper longing for God. If you assume that others love your brand the way you do, you are assuming a level of understanding that they may not have yet. Your role is to gently lead them along the path toward God, and you do that by interesting them in your brand, your work, and your ministry. If you assume that they already know and love your brand the way you do, you risk not connecting with them and potentially losing them.

You may remember the brand Healthy Choice. For a while it was all the rage, and the company's brand managers, thinking everyone loved their brand, quickly moved to introduce all sorts of product extensions. In short order, you could find Healthy Choice cookies, crackers, snacks, and frozen meals; the list grew exponentially. Unfortunately, it did not take long for the sales to plummet. What was Healthy Choice after all? Could it really be a cookie? Consumers were confused and walked away. They never loved the brand enough to invest the time, energy, and interest in figuring out what Healthy Choice was really all about. Fast-forward a

---

1. Mathew Sweezey, "The Future of Marketing 2016: New Roles and Trends," *Infinite Noise*, November 30, 2015, https://www.slideshare.net /MathewSweezey/the-future-of-marketing-2016-new-roles-tools-and-trends /15-InfiniteNoiseYankelovich_a_market_researchfirm_estimates.

few years, and today Healthy Choice is focused on healthier prepared meals in the frozen or refrigerated food sections. It's a brand people now understand.

Healthy Choice had great problems because they assumed everyone loved and understood the brand the way they did. As a result, the company moved faster than consumers liked, shifting and changing directions because they could see the possibilities. In the process they lost their consumers, who simply did not love the brand enough to go along for the ride.

Let's consider a faith-based example. Many parishes have a Eucharistic Adoration ministry. Have you ever talked to people who run that ministry at their parish? Typically, you will find that they absolutely love it — they love spending that quiet time with Christ in prayer. Many who have regular adoration times find these to be "no-skip" events. For those who have never participated in adoration, though, the excitement is much less clear. Often they simply don't understand. What do you do for an entire hour? Adoration is a simple example of this critical point in marketing. Those who participate absolutely love it. Those who do not participate do not understand it. We can talk about adoration for hours, but until you attend it yourself, you will never love it as much as someone who has already made it part of his or her life.

In St. Louis, there is a beautiful Carmelite monastery that has become an introduction to Eucharistic Adoration for many local Catholics. There, the Blessed Sacrament is exposed throughout each day, and people in the community are invited to stop by, if even for a minute or two. This gentle invitation encourages many to fall in love with adoration.

When it comes to your ministry, organization, or parish, do not worry if no one else loves it as you do quite yet. Stay true to your brand, stay consistent, and build it faithfully. If you are true to your brand and what it has to offer, people will come looking for it. Don't assume that people know and love it; invite them in slowly, interest them in the potential, and gently lead them. They may never love it as you do, but they will certainly need and appreciate it, and it will delight their hearts.

FOR REFLECTION

How can you share God's liberating love with those you care about without being pushy or overly dogmatic?

What is your response when someone is uninterested in pursuing spiritual growth or being on board with your mission?

Truth 4

EVERYONE NEEDS TO OWN THE BRAND

*"For just as the body is one and has many
members, and all the members of the body, though
many, are one body, so it is with Christ."*
— 1 CORINTHIANS 12:12

All too often, organizations have a sense that the brand is owned by one person or team — usually the marketing or communications team. Nothing could be further from the truth. Everyone in an organization has responsibility for the brand. Just as many parts make up one body, so all elements of an organization are part of the brand.

The reality that everyone owns the brand can be a very difficult concept. It does not mean that everyone is allowed to direct the brand; that truly needs to exist with marketing or communications. However, all members of an organization need to be committed to understanding the brand and delivering the brand message for their particular department. Organizations are used to having separate departments with a unique focus, such as finance, legal, human resources, operations, etc. However, every single one of these departments plays a role in communicating the company's brand.

An example of a brand that demonstrates well what happens when everyone owns the brand is Southwest Airlines. If you fly Southwest, you have probably heard a flight attendant sing or tell jokes to you over the plane's speaker. Most likely, the flight attendant understood the Southwest brand well enough to know that singing that particular ditty was a good thing to do. In other words, no one told the flight attendant to sing on Flight 2369 that morning. Instead, the flight attendant knows how to be a living example of the Southwest brand.

The reverse is true as well. I once worked with a pharmacy organization, and I couldn't understand why the pharmacists (the company's customers) were so vitriolic when speaking about the pharmacy corporation. I asked the pharmacists why they had such a strong reaction, and several complained about accounting. "Have you seen the notices they send us?" I looked at the accounting practices and, sure enough, the language was rough, coarse, and even mean. The pharmacy brand was about providing comforting support. These notices were inconsistent with what the brand claimed to stand for, and this was exceptionally irritating to the pharmacists. I worked with accounting to change the language in all the notices they sent to be consistent with the values of the brand. Over time, the pharmacists were no longer offended and became strong proponents of the brand.

A Catholic organization that takes brand seriously is the Fellowship of Catholic University Students. FOCUS trains young men and women just out of college to be missionaries on university campuses. One thing that will strike you when you meet a FOCUS missionary is his or her deep joy. Every single one of them demonstrates joy from faith, from God, and from this gift of life. Joy is hard to teach, as are many values and attitudes. FOCUS missionaries are hired in part for this attitude, as well as for their deep faith.

To hire for an attitude, you have to know what attitude or value you are seeking, which is where understanding your brand comes into play. FOCUS understands a few things about its brand:

1. Joy is central to the expression of the Catholic faith and, therefore, central to the role of their missionaries.
2. Members of FOCUS communicate the FOCUS brand and the call of the Gospel in how they approach and live their lives.

FOCUS recognizes that everyone in the organization plays a role in owning and expressing the brand. Each member of the organization is a part of the same body. At the same time, they recognize that their organization is part of the Body of Christ.

FOR REFLECTION

How do you express brand ownership as a member of the Body of Christ?

Do you see yourself as having an integral role in promoting the brand, especially if you work for a faith-based organization? Or do you sit back and let others lead the charge?

Truth 5

TO COMMUNICATE WELL, LESS IS MORE

"Better is a little that the righteous has
than the abundance of many wicked."
— PSALM 37:16

Have you ever wondered whether you should just do more when it comes to communications? If only you posted more on social media, sent more email marketing, planned more fundraising, more advertising, more promotions, more, more, more. It doesn't help that our society tells us that "more" is the answer to everything.

But what if I told you that the answer to achieving success is actually communicating less? It's true. When it comes to marketing, less is often more — much more. The problem with always doing more, more, more in communications is confusion and lack of focus. It is better to do a few things really well than many things poorly.

We see this in the business world quite a bit. Companies do well and then think their opportunity for further growth is to market differently or to communicate new messages. The secular world abounds with companies that, in the course of trying to communicate more, simply did damage to an already strong brand. Yahoo tried to redesign its logo in 2013 to freshen up the brand. They spent thirty days introducing various new logo options to their followers until the big unveiling of the new logo. An audible sigh went up in the marketing world when the new logo was released. It was not all that different. More importantly, Yahoo irritated its followers by pestering them with thirty different options over the course of thirty days. More communication was just that — more — and it caused more harm than good to the Yahoo brand at that time.

The fact that less is indeed more is a hard corporate lesson to learn. This lesson applies to many aspects of a ministry, parish, or religious organization. More communication, more emails, and more social media are often simply more. Challenge yourself with this question: what is your core message? What really needs to be shared? Are you communicating a lot simply to say you are doing so? Or are your messages clear and making a difference for those you want to reach?

Several women's religious orders provide an unfortunate example of how more is simply more. Several of the orders facing the fastest decline are hesitant to state their exact purpose. They indicate that they are serving social justice, which is outstanding, of course, but too broad. Are they serving the environment, the poor, the disenfranchised, education, sex trafficking, housing, impoverished nations? The list of possible activities is long, and they talk about all these options on their websites and in social media. These religious orders struggle to attract vocations, due in large part to the confusion caused by seeking to do more. They share a little of everything, and their fundamental message gets lost.

One such religious order shared with me that sisters are free to work for and support anything they see as a social justice issue. While the premise is noble, the result is that this order is not known or understood for anything in particular. Young women considering a vocation cannot figure out how they might fit in, what they would actually do, or how they would participate in social justice. With so many options, they simply walked away to another order with a distinct message — one doing less, but with greater clarity.

Many young women considering religious vocations seem to be turning to orders such as the Dominican Sisters of Mary, Mother of the Eucharist in Ann Arbor, Michigan. This order is newer, having been founded in 1997, and has more than 138 sisters as of this writing. Part of the attraction is the clarity and focus of their mission. Their website states, "Our apostolate follows upon preaching and teaching the Truth in order to gain souls for the Kingdom of Christ." They have a special devotion to Mary, the Mother of God, and to the Eucharist, and they make it clear that their apostolate flows from their prayer. They communicate well, and their message is direct; the results are clear.

This challenge of less is more plays out in marketing and communication constantly. When you do more social media or more email marketing, or more of anything, there is a natural inclination to change the message a bit. We don't want people to be bored or to get tired of what we say, so we shift it a little here and there. The next thing you know, those little shifts end up accumulating, and before long your message is off point.

More creates confusion. More is not necessarily clear. As written so superbly in the Book of Psalms (37:16), "better is a little that the righteous has." The solution is to strive for much and achieve that by doing less.

FOR REFLECTION

How would you define the core purpose of your organization or parish?

How does the push to do more distract you from your primary objectives?

Truth 6

A BRAND IS
A PROMISE

*"Woe to you, scribes and Pharisees, hypocrites! for
you are like whitewashed tombs, which outwardly
appear beautiful, but within they are full of dead
men's bones and all uncleanness. So you also outwardly appear righteous to men, but within you are
full of hypocrisy and iniquity."*
— MATTHEW 23:25–28

A brand is fundamentally a promise that you as market-ers, as communicators, are making to a consumer. As a promise, it has two parts: performance and perception. In the marketing world, we create perceptions that convey our promise. We then honor those commitments by what we do — our performance. Considered in light of the above verse from the Gospel of Matthew, perception can be likened to the outside of the cup. Performance can be seen as the inside of the cup.

Let's look at the inside first. Performance is what is

actually delivered — the product you make, the service you provide. So performance is also fundamentally what you deliver as a ministry, parish, or apostolate. How do you avoid making promises you cannot keep? I always advise that you start with what you do. Be really clear about what you provide. Remember, you don't have to do it all — you just need to do your part of God's work exceptionally well.

When you know what it is you do, that becomes your performance. Your next task is to create perceptions in the marketplace that reflect that performance. When the perceptions you create in the marketplace are aligned with your performance, then you have created a promise that you can keep. It really is that simple: do what you say you are going to do.

Now let's look at the outside of the cup. Perceptions are the messages that are created in the marketplace about the performance you provide. Let's take as an example an Energizer battery. Energizer's marketing team tells us that their battery is long-lasting. But if people were to buy their batteries, only to have them die the first time they were put into a device, then Energizer would have broken their promise that the battery would keep going and going. (Of course, I can tell you firsthand: Energizer does keep its promises, and its batteries are long lasting.)

The unfortunate reality is that human beings break promises all the time, and often not on purpose. As marketers working from a faith perspective, if we want to avoid breaking our promises, we have to be exceptionally diligent in understanding our performance. What do we say we can do? Can we always do that, meaning our promise can be trusted?

Bishop Robert Barron writes a daily morning reflection on the Gospel. I read it, and I love it. Bishop Barron promises that he will provide a Gospel reflection every day, and he does. Furthermore, his readers trust that each reflection will be filled with credible, faithful insights, fruits that we can use through the day; that is part of the promise. I don't know about you, but I am never disappointed. Bishop Barron keeps his promise.

As marketers and communicators, we create perceptions in the market as a way of conveying what we are promising. We create these perceptions through our advertising, social media, public relations, etc. The list is endless. We need to avoid creating a perception that is inconsistent with what we can actually do. If we create perceptions in the marketplace that we cannot deliver on, then we have broken our promise. Once our promise has been broken, it is very difficult for people to trust us again, whether we are individuals or brands.

Remember, when we're working for a faith-based organization, keeping our promises is even more important. When we are sharing promises about faith and God, we must honor those promises without fail. Standing firm and keeping our promises — especially in today's culture, where so many promises are broken — is radical. It stands out, and it will cause people to take notice and listen.

This fundamental brand truth — that a brand is a promise — calls to mind the message Christ gave to the Pharisees. It is not enough to clean the outside of the cup; they must clean the inside as well. Cleaning a cup so that it is beautiful on the outside doesn't matter if the inside is a mess, just as creating wonderful perceptions is irrelevant if you do not perform as promised. Your brand is your promise; make sure you keep it.

FOR REFLECTION

What promise does your brand make?

How do you and your colleagues keep that promise?

Truth 7

PRICE IS THE COMMUNICATION OF YOUR VALUE

*"And a poor widow came, and put in two
copper coins, which make a penny. And he
called his disciples to him, and said to them,
'Truly, I say to you, this poor widow has put
in more than all those who are contributing to
the treasury. For they all contributed out of their
abundance; but she out of her poverty has put in
everything she had, her whole living.'"*
— MARK 12:42–44

While the poor widow in the Gospel did not have much money, she greatly valued the faith to which she was contributing. She so valued it that she offered two coins, "her whole livelihood." There is a lot we can take from this message in terms of how we value our products and services. Are you offering goods and services of value? I suspect so.

43

In that case, understand that your price is simply the communication of that value.

When sharing faith-filled messages, the tendency is to provide much for free, or really, really cheap. Granted, we need to reach as many people as possible, and free appears to do that. But let me push back on that a little bit, because this argument confuses reach and content. Reach is how we get to many people, and there are ways of doing this that are quite inexpensive, especially given social media. Content, however, is the knowledge, platform, information, service, and products you provide. That content has value.

You have worked, you have prayed, you have listened, you have studied, you have done a great deal to create a brand that communicates faith in God. That work, that knowledge does have value, and you need to communicate that value.

Price defines value. So, when you price something low, you are suggesting that the value is low. Pricing represents your own perceptions of your brand. Think about cars: a BMW is priced far higher than a Kia. The perception created is that the BMW has greater value, and that it performs better than the Kia. BMW has stipulated that by their price; and Kia has concurred, based on their price. We, as consumers, see the pricing and intuitively understand the difference.

Whether we like it or not, pricing creates differentiation in the mind of the consumer. In a world that is driven by money, defining value for your product or service is critical, for that is how human beings are trained to understand things.

Imagine a Catholic radio station that has been in business for years, sharing faith-based programming. They have discovered many of the day's leading Catholic speakers. Yet they never pay for their speakers. Moreover, they have few sponsors for their programs. Many speakers get started with them and then quickly leave. Speakers leave because the lack of payment and sponsors indicates that the station does not value their message. If the station's leadership doesn't value their message, why should anyone else?

Yet, in the faith-based world, this use of "free" is common. Speakers will say they speak for free. People will give out their books or products for free. I am not suggesting that you overprice your products, books, or speeches. I am saying that people will value them more when you value them. People need to understand that what you are saying, doing, and writing matters. In our society, the way people understand that value is in the price they pay.

The poor widow who gave the two coins to the temple so valued the Lord that she wanted to give everything she had to him, even though it was little. I share this story because it speaks to value. People recognize value by what they pay. Help them know that you are sharing elements of faith that have value by pricing your work appropriately, remembering that your price is the communication of your value.

FOR REFLECTION

Have you struggled with how much to charge for your services?

How might this reflect on the value that you place on what you do? And how might this influence how others perceive what you are offering?

BRANDS ARE INFLUENCED BY THE ASSOCIATIONS THEY KEEP

*"He who walks with wise men becomes wise,
but the companion of fools will suffer harm."*
— Proverbs 13:20

We have all heard the old adage that we are known by the company we keep. That is very true for brands as well. People begin to learn of, understand, and appreciate your brand based on your brand's close associations. Therefore, managing those associations is critical to managing your brand. Associations can serve as shortcuts to help a customer understand who and what you are.

Let's start by considering a secular example. In the beer industry, Budweiser is known as the King of Beers. It is associated with the grand Clydesdale horses. It is seen as a favorite beverage for sporting events such as baseball games. Each of these is an association that influences our opinion of the Budweiser brand.

In the corporate world, those associations are carefully managed. I remember vividly that when I worked with Energizer, there was a camera company all but begging to do a joint promotion with us. Our answer was no, because they were an unknown entity. They replied, "That is why we want to partner with you, so that others will learn of us." The risk for Energizer was that they might not hold the same values we did. What if they did not treat customers as we did? Associations matter for all involved, and they must be considered carefully.

In our Catholic world, we have been given some spectacular associations that we can use and depend on from the very start in any ministry, faith-based business, or parish. Mary comes to mind as a beautiful example. Jesus gives his mother to us, as we read in the Gospel, and what a powerful association that is. We can settle in the embrace of Mary's love, knowing that through her we are directly connected to Christ when doubt sets in. Mary, in embracing us, encourages us as we bring forward her Son's work. That association supports us as we proceed in doing the Father's work.

We find associations all throughout our faith. Simply look at the religious orders. The associations of the founder influence the entire order. Franciscans today still have a love of creation, the earth, animals, and peace that seamlessly relate back to Saint Francis and his love of these things. That association, because it is used consistently, quickly conveys the promise of Franciscan orders today.

Another lovely example is the rosary, those simple beads that are so deeply meaningful. As Catholics, the Rosary is a profound, blessed prayer for us. Many of us grip the string of beads tightly when life is difficult, we hold it to our heart in thanksgiving, and we keep it nearby in a pocket or purse at all times. When we see others using those beads, we know that they pray, that they are Catholic, and that they turn to Mother Mary as a beautiful intercessor with God.

When it comes to building and sharing our brand, association work must be intentional work. We must think about it, reflect on it, pray about it, and then identify those people and those elements of our Catholic faith that are most closely aligned with our mission, ministry, or parish. You don't need to have lots of associations. You need to have a few that are profound and speak to the essence of your organization.

Associations can take a variety of forms. They can include the words that are said or the colors that are used. Ever notice how many times that beautiful shade of blue is used with Mary? Just that color demonstrates an association with Mary for many of us.

The trick with associations is that once they are identified, they need to be used consistently. Associations can help a customer's brain to more quickly think of you, your brand, and your organization. But that relationship will not be understood if the associations are not applied in a consistent manner. In fact, it is better to have a few clear associations that are consistently used than a bunch that are haphazardly utilized.

Are you familiar with Word on Fire, the Catholic ministry that supports Bishop Barron with a mission to use media to draw people back to the Faith? Even seeing the words here, you can probably visualize the "fire" that is part of their logo. In fact, the image of fire is critical to them and to the message they are sharing. That flame represents the Holy Spirit as well as an urgency, an emphasis, a burning desire for God. The association with that simple flame communicates so much for this expanding and impactful ministry. Your brand's relevance and differentiation can be clearly conveyed through associations as well, but only when done consistently.

One example of the impact associations can have is the public grief over the devastating fire in Notre Dame Cathedral in Paris, which started on April 15, 2019, as this book neared publication. As the flames began destroying the cathedral, people flooded the streets of Paris singing the "Ave Maria." Notre Dame is not just a historic French treasure, it is a central landmark of Catholicism, a holder of critical relics, and a profound symbol of our faith. The magnificent cathedral's burning felt personal to people all over the world and in France, because its many rich associations have made it feel like it belongs to each one of us.

Be intentional as you identify associations. If you are considering associations from the Bible, or with saints, then keep studying them. When looking to associations for insights, find lines of sight between what they do and how that connects to what you do.

FOR REFLECTION

Is there a saint, biblical character, or sacramental that connects to the essence of your work and service? How do you reinforce that association, or what steps can you take to do so?

How can these associations help people better understand your mission?

Truth 9

THE CUSTOMER EXPERIENCE IS THE BRAND EXPERIENCE

"And Levi made him a great feast in his house;
and there was a large company of tax collectors
and others sitting at table with them."
— LUKE 5:29

In this verse from Luke, it is striking that a large crowd of tax collectors was gathered at this banquet. Respectable people at that time would never associate with tax collectors; yet here was Christ, eating with them. Imagine the experience the tax collectors were having at this meal! They were experiencing faith directly, from Christ himself. What about those who were not tax collectors? What were they experiencing as they watched Christ sit and dine with the tax collectors?

The experience is critical for a customer. The experience customers have becomes their view of the brand. They will convey their perspectives of the brand based on the experiences they have. You can tell them all you want about your brand — you can share who you are, provide key messages, etc. — but if you act differently, what they will recall is your action.

There are teams of people in corporate boardrooms whose sole role is to make sure the customer's experience with their brand is consistent with the values of their brand.

Consider two examples. The Chipotle brand has fallen on rough times as of late. The company used to be known for outstanding Mexican food. Then, severe bouts of food poisoning occurred at several of their restaurants. The customer experience of getting sick is now closely aligned with the Chipotle brand. Even if the food is great, and the problem is corrected, those negative customer experiences have defined the brand for many people.

On the other hand, Chick-fil-A is a favorite fast-food restaurant for many people these days. A study recently explained that part of why everyone loves Chick-fil-A is because the people who work there say "please" and "thank you."[2] Simply using basic manners is enough to influence the customer experience and, therefore, the brand experience.

Now think about the parish you attend. Does your priest greet everyone after Mass? What type of experience is that providing to parishioners as well as the broader community? I have family in a small town in Ohio, and the pastor of the parish there is well known for his deep connection with everyone. After Mass, he waits outside the front of the church and chats with people as they leave.

2. Kate Taylor, "Chick-fil-A Is Beating Every Competitor by Training Workers to Say 'Please' and 'Thank You,'" *Business Insider*, October 3, 2016, https://www.businessinsider.com/chick-fil-a-is-the-most-polite-chain-2016-10. See also Alicia Kelso, "Chick-fil-A Is Now McDonald's Biggest Threat," *Forbes*, December 20, 2018, https://www.forbes.com/sites/aliciakelso/2018/12/20/how-chick-fil-a-positioned-itself-to-be-mcdonalds-biggest-threat/#3f20f9c41ae7.

This pastor is known throughout the broader community as well. You don't have to be Catholic, or even from his neighborhood, to feel the love. He is known throughout the city and loved by many. He provides an experience of deep relationships and community in the area. The manner in which "customers" experience him and his parish directly influences their understanding of Catholicism in this small town.

Think about the many ways you touch your customers, from those who are active in a ministry, to those doing the communications or marketing, to those in development or finance. Every single interaction is an opportunity to create a customer experience and, therefore, a brand experience. Are those interactions consistent with the brand you are trying to communicate? If not, what must change in the customer's experience of you?

What will you do? Will you set the banquet table for the tax collectors, as described in Luke 5:29? Will you provide them unique brand experiences that only your ministry, your parish, your organization can provide? When you provide that customer experience, what will others learn from you? Christ sat and dined with tax collectors, providing the experience that he was sent by the Father and was there for everyone, not just the few. What customer experience can you provide?

FOR REFLECTION

What are the most important ways in which you interact with your customers?

How could you improve the overall unique customer experience you provide?

Truth 10

EGO MEANS "DANGER AHEAD"

"When pride comes, then comes disgrace;
but with the humble is wisdom."
— Proverbs 11:2

It is all too easy to let ego drive what we do. That is true for individuals and true for organizations. When an organization's ego is the driver, the consumer or user is forgotten. As Proverbs says so clearly, with pride comes disgrace. From a brand and marketing perspective, the sentiment holds true as well; for when pride occurs, the disgrace for the organization can be exceptionally damaging.

When an organization works from a place of ego, the focus shifts away from the user or consumer. As a result, those who run the organization begin to believe they can do more than they truly can. They make promises they are unable to keep, and they care less about the customer experience and more about their own accolades. They fall into a pit where they are so self-focused that they often don't even realize that people are leaving them for something else.

A few years ago, Zippo, the lighter brand, decided to create Zippo ladies' perfume. It flopped massively and is a great example of corporate ego getting in the way.[3] While those who are fans of Zippo are very committed, the attempt to translate that into perfume caused the marketing world to shake its collective head.

When we build a brand or market or communicate our work, we are trying to share our message with someone else. The best way to share our information is to start by understanding the consumer to whom we are speaking. Who is our customer and what matters to them? When our organizational ego gets in the mix, we neglect our customer's voice. Worse yet, we think we know better than the customer.

When an organization has a strong ego, not only can the customer perspective be lost, but other critical disconnects occur. As Proverbs points out, disgrace often follows pride. Sure enough, we often see that with ego comes greed for more and more money, taking the focus away from the ministry and the good work to be done. With ego comes boasting and pride, which puts the focus on ourselves or the ministry instead of on the people we claim to serve. Because of ego, we sometimes find people resorting to unethical practices or making outrageous claims.

Humility is a central call of the Gospel. For without humility, we are unable to focus and serve others well. This is true for organizations as much as it is true for individuals. While your parish, ministry, or organization may be doing outstanding work in your community, do not let that go to your head. Do not fall into the trap of thinking you can do it all. Rather, stay humble and keep your focus on those you

---

3. "Branding Basics #14: The Law of Sub-Brands," *Agenda*, May 4, 2016, https://www.agendamarketing.ca/branding-basics-14-law-of-sub-brands/.

serve. Keep Proverbs 11:2 in mind: remember that with your humility comes wisdom.

FOR REFLECTION

In what areas are you tempted to do it all, feeling that no one can do it better than you?

Where does ego creep in and dilute your focus?

Truth 11

BRAND METRICS ARE THE BEST MEASURE OF SUCCESS

"And David had success in all his
undertakings; for the Lord was with him."
— 1 SAMUEL 18:14

M ost organizations are very focused on achieving success. Often, that success is measured in revenue, donations, and anything else that makes up the financial side of the organizational equation. There is no denying that money is important for the operations of a parish, mission, or ministry. However, money is not typically the best measure of success.

When dealing with brands, there are other measures of success that are more critical. The first of such measures is awareness. It simply speaks to whether communities or markets are aware of you as an entity. In the corporate world, there are varying levels of awareness, including aided, unaided, and top-of-mind awareness. Aided awareness occurs when your organization or ministry name is mentioned, and the customer recognizes the name. Unaided awareness occurs when you provide no prompts, and the customer can simply pull your name out of memory. Top-of-mind awareness is the highest form of awareness, and it indicates that of all the possibilities, your ministry or organizational name was the first to come to a customer's mind.

Awareness is critical, because if someone is not aware of you, it is virtually impossible for them to choose or use you. But awareness is not the only metric to watch. Another critical measure is called preference. Preference addresses whether you are the preferred solution to the customer's need. It is possible to have a great deal of awareness, but not be preferred by a customer.

Consider the simple bar soap. You know many of the names: Ivory, Irish Spring, Dial. Yet, while most customers are aware of these soaps, they do not actually prefer them. Consumers often prefer to use other soaps; typically soaps that are gentler, have a better fragrance, or are richer and more emollient. These are the preferred brands.

For parishes, missions, ministries, and organizations, you need to work to build awareness so that people know you. Secondly, you need to work to build preference, so that you are their primary choice when they are looking for your faith-based service or product.

When we think about brand metrics for the Catholic Church, one of the most basic is the number of people attending Mass. We know the numbers have declined significantly. The CARA report on adult Catholics shows staggering numbers of adult Catholics leaving the church. At the same time, we see an enormous increase in the number of people joining Protestant megachurches. The preference for these megachurches is high, even though there is great awareness of Catholicism and the Catholic Church.

What drives people from simply being aware to preferring a particular church? Many of the people attending megachurches are drawn to the community, the entertainment factor, the consumerism aspect, or (in many cases) an inspirational leader. "The cultural norms and values have changed in that most of our institutions are no longer small and antiquated with organs and wooden pews," says Scott Thumma, a leading expert in megachurch research and professor of sociology religion at the Hartford Institute. "It's not surprising that the religious life parallels and echoes everyday life."[4]

Megachurches have been successful at driving preference based on familiarity. People recognize in these churches what they experience in society. What can we learn from this in our Catholic churches? What our churches offer isn't more secular activities, but the Holy Eucharist (the source and summit of our faith). Everything else flows from there. When we bring people into our faith, and they experience the Holy Eucharist, we are inviting them to a deeper level of preference, a yearning for God. As that preference builds, it is profound for them and not based on superficial secular experiences.

Consider the Society of St. Vincent de Paul, a well-known organization dedicated to serving the poor. Many parishes have an arm of St. Vincent de Paul that engages parishioners in the support of the poor in their community. This organization has both great awareness and great preference. Virtually every Catholic you interact with will be aware

---

4. Amanda Sakuma, "The Super-Sized Growth Behind Megachurches," MSNBC, October 24, 2014, http://www.msnbc.com/msnbc/the-super-sized-growth-behind-megachurches.

of the organization. Many people also prefer to support it. When there is a choice about where to donate gently used clothes or furniture, or where to make a financial donation, St. Vincent de Paul is at the top of the list. When there is a question of how to serve the poor more directly, individuals participate in St. Vincent de Paul ministries.

What makes St. Vincent de Paul such a great example for us is that their focus is on the right thing: their service to the poor. Because they stay true to their mission, people are aware of the work they do and prefer to support them in a variety of ways. Their great success is measured by how many lives they touch.

The thing is, if you are preferred, the money will follow. People use, support, and donate to those organizations they prefer. The best measure of success, therefore, is not necessarily the dollars you collect but rather measurements about your brand, its awareness and preference. Samuel's verse resounds well for us in that David had success "for the Lord was with him."

FOR REFLECTION

How can you increase awareness about the work that you do, so people immediately think of you? What makes you unique?

What are some ways you can strengthen the way you present your faith message so that your followers are attracted to you and what you offer?

Truth 12

COMPLAINTS ARE JEWELED TREASURES FROM YOUR CUSTOMER

"Now in these days when the disciples were increasing in number, the Hellenists murmured against the Hebrews because their widows were neglected in the daily distribution. And the Twelve summoned the body of the disciples. ... And the word of God increased; and the number of the disciples multiplied greatly in Jerusalem."
— ACTS 6:1-2,7

It is always fascinating to see how terrified organizations are of complaints. Customer satisfaction is often measured every step of the way with the goal of always getting high satisfaction numbers. The organizations that get it right, however, understand that it can be good to hear complaints from customers.

Complaints are truly treasures. They provide much insight, from what is working within an organization to what matters to customers, to what new options may make sense for a product or service. Sure, it is difficult to hear complaints. But it is even more difficult to see your organization fail to thrive, especially when your customers were more than willing to tell you what the issues were.

When I was leading the marketing at a retail division of Cardinal Health, we started receiving complaints from one particular customer who used our private label body lotion. She complained that her cat liked to lick her arms, but was now getting sick. Something must have changed with the lotion, she thought, since the cat was getting sick every time he licked her arm. While there was quite a bit of laughter about this one, our astute director of product marketing started asking questions. What if the formula had changed? Sure enough, it had, and the manufacturer had neglected to tell us. Because of that complaint, the product director changed the business processes around product agreements, so that the organization was aware of even the slightest change and could communicate that to all customers. Additionally, the customer received lots of the previous formula as a thank you for letting us know.

It takes quite a bit of humility to accept and truly listen to customer complaints. Land's End does this exceptionally well. They truly want customers to be happy. So, if a customer has a return or any issue, they gratefully handle it. Their only request is that the customer explain the problem. When their next catalog comes out, it is not uncommon to see changes to products based on customer feedback.

One has to wonder how different things might be for the Catholic Church if the leaders who heard the early complaints about abuse had taken action. When leaders hear complaints, they are better able to understand the significance and correct the situation. Customer complaints are a treasure when organizations act on them. To receive complaints and then do nothing is a sure way to erode your brand, your message, and your image. Again, the abuse crisis in the Catholic Church demonstrates this loudly. Complaints were made and not addressed, and we are living with the result.

In Acts 6, the Hellenist members of the early Church complained because their widows were not receiving as much assistance as the Hebrew widows were. In response to these complaints, the Church instituted the diaconate. Today, deacons continue to perform a vital role in the Church — and all because the Apostles were willing to listen to complaints. This is a great reminder as you build your faith-based organization or brand. There are jeweled treasures within the complaints you receive, if you are willing to listen and learn from them.

FOR REFLECTION

Think of some negative feedback you've received. How did you perceive it — and how did you respond?

Describe a time when a complaint ended up being a "treasure" and improved your organization.

Truth 13

BRAND STEWARDSHIP STARTS WITH YOU

"He who is faithful in a very little is faithful also in much; and he who is dishonest in a very little is dishonest also in much."

— LUKE 16:10

We all know the adage that raising a child with strong values begins at home. The same is true for your brand. Your brand's "home" is your organization, and how you manage your brand at home will influence how it is perceived in the community. Every part of the brand that you manage — the promise, logo, name, message, all of the various elements — starts with you. Your organization, your team, your leadership, your communications and event partners — you are the drivers of your brand.

The verse above from Luke resonates so clearly as we think about brands. "He who is faithful in a very little is faithful also in much." From a brand perspective, this means being true to the details of the brand. The logo and color palette must remain consistent. The messaging should be on point. If the littlest things change or are inconsistent, what does that mean for the bigger elements, such as the service you provide, the products you offer, or your development efforts?

The other critical element here is leadership. Being committed to your marketing, your communication, your brand, starts at the top. If leadership is not committed, why should the rest of the organization be committed? If the organization is not committed, then why should the consumer or user care? Every member of an organization plays a role in delivering the promise of the organization. Too many times, organizations defer to marketing or communications to manage the messaging, the promise, and the brand. However, effective stewardship means that everyone takes the brand to heart, such that the promise reaches deeply into the organization and becomes a natural way for the organization to work and behave.

A favorite example of outstanding brand stewardship is Donatos Pizza. This regional pizza chain from Columbus, Ohio, had this tagline for years: "Respect the Pizza." A few years back, a group of people ordered Donatos pizza for a party. The delivery guy asked whether everyone had plates. "No, but we have napkins," was the reply. "Respect the pizza," he responded, and he handed over a stack of sturdy paper plates. Stewardship of Donatos brand occurs from leadership all the way through the organization to the delivery guy, ensuring that the brand and promise, along with the pizza, are respected.

Consider Saint Paul and what this great apostle did for the growth and spread of Catholicism. He embodied the fact that stewardship begins with you. Once he underwent his conversion, he lived zealously, carrying the message of

Christ to different continents and to everyone he met. From little conversations with individuals, to his letters, to his preaching and speaking, Saint Paul was trusted in the small matters as well as the large matters to share the good news of Christ. Paul was relentless, and that paved the way for the spread of the Faith.

Stewarding your brand effectively requires deep understanding of your brand. When the promise, the messages, the rationales for your brand's creative are well understood, they can be effectively applied to every detail of the organization. When they are applied consistently to the little things, people know that the brand can be trusted for the big things.

The message from Luke 16:10, "He who is faithful in a very little is faithful also in much," is an important message for us as individuals and for the organizations that are trying to do God's work on earth.

FOR REFLECTION

What are some "little things" you've been entrusted with?

How can attention to detail lead to bigger opportunities for what you're seeking to accomplish for the kingdom?

Truth 14

FOCUSED, SIMPLE, AND CLEAR: THE CORNERSTONES OF YOUR ORGANIZATION'S WORK

"Let your eyes look directly forward,
and your gaze be straight before you.
Take heed to the path of your feet,
then all your ways will be sure."
— PROVERBS 4:25–26

It is so tempting to try to do many different things. You see the need; you suspect you can fulfill it; and before long, your organization is doing lots of things...but very few well. It is difficult to discipline ourselves to stay focused on our central purpose; yet, for an organization and for a brand, it is critical.

How many times do we hear someone yell out "Squirrel!"

joking about how dogs chase every squirrel they see? This image aptly describes organizations and individuals chasing too many initiatives. What are your squirrels? How can you avoid the temptations and stay focused?

There are a few reasons why being focused in your work is important. First of all, no one organization can do everything well. Being focused ensures that you are doing the work in which you truly excel. This does not mean you won't see other needs that should be addressed. It does mean that you make very conscious decisions to let other organizations address those needs, because you cannot do it all.

The second reason that focus is important is because it makes it easier for your consumers or users to understand what you do. The amount of information that consumers are bombarded with each day is staggering. People, generally speaking, cannot effectively process all the messaging they receive each day. Certainly, they are not motivated by each and every item. So, if you add to that clutter by sharing multitudes of services you provide, you are also adding to confusion for them. As Proverbs states, "Let your eyes look directly forward, and your gaze be straight before you." When your gaze is focused forward, your consumers will focus forward as well.

With focus comes simplicity. When you remove all the extraneous squirrels, then the activities you undertake, the messages you convey all become simpler, and that is easier for a consumer to process. Focus leads to simplicity, which leads to clarity for those you are trying to reach.

How do you find focus, simplicity, and clarity for your brand? It starts with clearly defining your brand promise. The brand promise should reflect the people you are trying to reach, what makes you unique, and what values you bring forward. In Truth 6 we spent time addressing your brand promise, which includes the performance of your organization and the perceptions created. Being focused, simple, and clear about your performance, or what you actually do, is critical. The discipline comes in saying no to items that are not consistent with your brand promise, with what you say you deliver.

Consider the Holy Spirit Adoration Sisters, a cloistered contemplative community of nuns. They are known for their prayerfulness and for being immersed in Christ, most specifically through perpetual adoration. Their habits are pink, and thus they are colloquially known as the Pink Sisters. If there is a personal or worldwide challenge, people know to ask the Pink Sisters to pray. They have generated interest, support, and followers because of their prayerfulness. Because of this interest, they have surely faced many opportunities to branch out, do more, do something different. Yet they say no and keep their focus on the thing they do best: prayer. As a result, the external world clearly understands that these are women of great prayerfulness and faith.

Now consider your own ministry or faith-based organization. What is the path for your feet? Where are your eyes focused as you consider your ministry? Be sure to focus forward so that your work and, as a result, your messaging can be simple and clear.

FOR REFLECTION

Write a concise statement expressing the central focus of your organization.

What are two ways you could hone your focus so your message is crystal clear?

Truth 15

MARKETING IS COURTSHIP

*"Search out and seek, and she will become known to
you; and when you get hold of her, do not let her go."*
— SIRACH 6:27

The point of marketing is to connect your ministry, your
parish, your good work with others. Marketing is an
invitation for them to participate with you. Unfortunately,
too many times in the secular world, there is the sense that
marketing is "war." I cannot begin to tell you how wrong that
metaphor is. Effective marketing is the complete opposite of
war; in fact, it is courtship.

A war-driven concept is very much a competitor-
focused approach. Secular companies see themselves as
fighting with competitors (such as the Coke vs. Pepsi wars).
Even as you read the word *war*, you may tense up. You think
of strength and domination, gamesmanship, perhaps even
lawlessness — getting whatever you can at whatever cost.
The issue with this approach is that it takes our eyes off what

really matters: the customer.

A courtship, on the other hand, is all about trying to search out and seek or "woo" someone to join you, to be a part of your ministry, to be a customer of yours. This approach understands deeply what matters to your customer and takes the time to share how your service, parish, or ministry will meet the needs they express. This does not happen immediately, but over time — just like a courtship.

Spending time getting to know customers allows you to understand more fully their needs. Of course, there are multiple technical ways to get to know them, including surveys, focus groups, market research, promotions, and trial programs — the list is seemingly endless. Yet the spirit of courtship is to enter into a long-term relationship. For a faith-based organization, the best way to get to know the customer is to use the method that Christ showed us: to invest deeply in a few people, as he did when he called his apostles.

One organization that does this exceptionally well is FOCUS (the Fellowship of Catholic University Students mentioned in Truth 4). FOCUS places recent college graduates on college campuses to work as missionaries among the students. FOCUS does not ask their missionaries to work with hundreds of students, however. Instead, they ask each missionary to invest in just a few students, with an intention of developing deep relationships with the few rather than superficial relationships with hundreds of students.

In 2009, FOCUS had a few missionaries at twenty universities. Those missionaries were working with several students each. Fast forward to 2019, and FOCUS will have more than 690 missionaries walking with thousands of college students around the country.[5] That is thousands of deep

5. FOCUS 2018 Annual Report, available at https://www.focus.org/about/annual -reports.

relationships centered on God, all because of the courtship of FOCUS missionaries.

Yes, you can do lots of research and gain many insights about your potential customers, and that is certainly helpful. However, your long-term relationship must be based on more than simply research-based knowledge. You need to understand what matters to your customers. You need to share information, services, insights, and products that answer their needs. You need to listen to them.

The essence of marketing is to attract customers who will benefit from what you have to offer. You are seeking to build righteous, holy partnerships. As a faith-based organization, your strategy should not be war, but courtship. This strategy will lead you to customers, and it will draw customers into deep relationship with you. After all, God is love, and courtship is your marketing path to bring people to God.

FOR REFLECTION

What are some ways you currently "court" those you serve?

What are some practical ways you might develop deeper relationships with those you seek to reach?

Truth 16

FOCUS ON MISSION IS MORE VALUABLE THAN FOCUS ON FUNDING

*"As for what was sown on good soil, this is
he who hears the word and understands it; he
indeed bears fruit, and yields, in one case a
hundredfold, in another sixty, and in another thirty."*
— MATTHEW 13:23

Funding is critical; there is no denying that. However, losing your focus in the chase for additional dollars will do a disservice to your mission, parish, or organization, and to your brand. All too often, energy is spent in trying to increase donations, drive sales, or generate funding.

In the corporate world, when sales decline, management springs into action, often identifying new items or services that the organization can offer. They will do anything to revitalize sales. Do you remember the Limited clothing retail chain? It used to be a favorite of young women. It featured contemporary styles that were reasonably priced. Sales pressures caused the retailer to expand to additional audiences. The Limited, in a fight for growth, lost its focus. It had too many styles and tried to reach too many different people, all in search of that almighty dollar. In 2017, the retailer announced that it was closing all its stores.

For faith-based organizations, it is natural to suppose that if sales, donations, or funding are weak, then doing more should increase the dollars. The problem with doing more is that this usually means being less focused. It is counterintuitive, but doing more, instead of helping, actually hurts your efforts. Matthew's message of sowing a seed in rich soil rings especially true here. If you stay focused on what you know and do well, you will do even more with that message you share.

This can be a challenge when leading a not-for-profit ministry, organization, or parish. It is common to have a donor specify a particular project or building improvement. It is tempting to say yes, as the money is helpful, and you don't want to irritate a donor. However, if saying yes causes you to spend time and energy on something that is not closely aligned to your mission, you may see a short-term financial boost for a long-term mission challenge. Mission "creep" is a real thing, and causes real problems.

Consider as well the priest abuse scandal the Church is struggling with currently. A common response by lay Catholics trying to get the attention of leaders is that they will pull their funding. That message of pulling funding is a tangible way of expressing their deep disappointment in the Church over this crisis.

Stories like this abound, because mission and funding are inextricably linked. When money is on the line, it is easy not to notice when the work, programs, or efforts are inconsistent with a brand's focus. The money is too enticing, so organizations decide they will make it work. However, making it work may be far more costly than anticipated.

Instead, focus on your mission, on providing your services, and on providing them well. Don't lose your focus in your chase for funding, for those seeds are often sown on dry or thorny soil. Rather, sow your seeds in rich soil, tend them carefully, and don't sacrifice focus for revenue. Your rich soil is the primary focus of your organization, and the only soil that will bear fruit.

FOR REFLECTION

What kinds of issues cause you to lose your focus when it comes to your particular calling?

Have you ever said yes to funding that was inconsistent with your mission? What was the result?

Truth 17

IT IS NOT THE MEDIUM; IT IS THE MESSAGE

"And we have the prophetic word made more sure.
You will do well to pay attention to this as to a
lamp shining in a dark place, until the day dawns
and the morning star rises in your hearts."
— 2 PETER 1:19

Canadian Catholic professor Marshall McLuhan wrote the oft-quoted line, "The medium is the message." While McLuhan was pointing out that each medium affects the very way in which we think about the messages received through that medium, the phrase is often used colloquially to suggest that the medium is more important than the message. And that can lead marketers to downplay the importance of crafting a clear message.

Consider the annual Super Bowl. For big brands, a TV ad during the Super Bowl is the ultimate medium in which to share their message. That one game draws millions of viewers around the world, but especially in the United States.

The biggest brands are able to purchase what is typically the most expensive advertising of the year. In 2018, a thirty-second Super Bowl ad cost an advertiser $5 million. Yes, you read that right: $5 million for one thirty-second advertisement. Do you remember any of the ads from 2018?

Typically, Budweiser, Coca-Cola, and Doritos will spend the big bucks for Super Bowl advertising. In 2018, you also saw ads for Amazon's Alexa, Tide, Groupon, and Kia, among others. Are any of these ringing a bell? Probably not. Yes, Super Bowl ads reach millions of people, but very few of us actually remember them later. This raises the question: was it worthwhile to spend that $5 million?

Few Super Bowl ads are really remembered. One of the most famous ever was the 1984 Apple ad for the launch of its Macintosh computer. MasterLock is also remembered for its Super Bowl advertising, though the company did run the same ad several years in a row. (In the ad, someone shoots a rifle at the lock, but the padlock holds.) Other than those two, there are few memorable Super Bowl ads. So why do companies spend so much money on the Super Bowl? Because they believe that "the medium is the message," so a splashy Super Bowl ad should have a profound impact on consumers.

In our day and age, there are a number of mediums — from traditional print, radio, and TV, to websites and online advertising, to social media. Yet think about it: If you put lots of "stuff" on social media but do not have a clear message, it will not connect with your potential users. A great example of someone who understood this very well was Bishop Fulton Sheen. He had a great message that he shared in a variety of ways, but his focus was always on his message, not on the medium. This is important to remember. The various mediums are simply delivering your message — they are not the message. So the critical issue is, what is your message?

People are attentive to your message, not necessarily the means by which you share that message. Regardless of your organization's specific activities, most likely your message ultimately invites people to form a closer relationship with God, and that is a prophetic message. Be attentive to your message, the light you are sharing, so that the morning star can rise in the hearts of those you serve.

FOR REFLECTION

How do you invite people to form a closer relationship with God?

What mediums do you use, and how do these serve your message?

Truth 18

POSITIONING LIVES IN THE MIND OF YOUR AUDIENCE

*"As Jesus passed on from there, he saw a man
called Matthew sitting at the tax office; and he said
to him, 'Follow me.' And he rose and followed him.
And as he sat at table in the house, behold, many tax
collectors and sinners came and sat down with Jesus
and his disciples. And when the Pharisees saw this,
they said to his disciples, 'Why does your teacher
eat with tax collectors and sinners?'"*
— MATTHEW 9:9–11

Have you ever tried to change someone's mind about something? We know from experience that our opinions are deeply ingrained in our brains. This is clear in the Gospel passage quote above. The Pharisees could not get past their preconceived notions of tax collectors.

Consider this now in the context of your brand. Where

does your brand live? Most often, organizations believe the brand exists in the retail store or in the experience created by the service. Yet in reality, your brand — its positioning or role in the world — lives in the user's mind. While that may seem odd, it is, in fact, very true.

Customers get to know your brand and its position through their experience with your product or service. Just as Matthew was known for collecting taxes, people know your brand by what you do and what is said about you.

All too often, organizations talk about changing their brand or repositioning their brand. They seem to believe that by creating a new logo or a different tagline, they are well on the way to changing their brand the way they see fit. Alas, it does not work that way. Unless you change someone's mind about your brand or your position, the new creative will never make a difference. In the end, the logo, the tagline, etc., are mere symbols for your customers and consumers. Their brains will remember the brands as they know them, and that is exceedingly difficult to change.

For years and years, Sears has valiantly tried to reposition itself, to change its brand. Remember the once-great Sears catalog and how you could even purchase a ready-made house? Yet now, years later, few people have ever actually seen that catalog. So it is with a brand. No matter how hard Sears tries, as far as consumers are concerned, they are the old catalog company. No amount of store refreshing, advertising, or promotion has been able to substantially shift the image the customers have of Sears.

People's opinions live in their minds. If you are trying to reposition your organization or ministry and to change people's minds about it, you will need to break through all of the other things going on in their brain, and remind them vigorously of your new position. It is not easy, for remember that you are just one of the many brands they consider each day. It is so much easier for someone to remember who you used to be.

That does not mean it cannot be done, however. It just means that great diligence will be needed to make a real change. It must be repeated over and over again and lived precisely the way you want it known for someone's understanding of your brand to change. It is always best to spend a bit more time up front deciding on a brand position than to try to change it later.

Christ worked to change the position of Matthew and tax collectors when he invited Matthew to follow him. Because Matthew was called by and was constantly with Christ, he began to lose the mantle of tax collector and become known as a disciple. He is now known for his Gospel, though we also know that he was once a tax collector. How difficult it is to change a position in people's minds.

FOR REFLECTION

How would someone describe what you do? How accurate is their perception?

How can you help people to have a different perspective when it comes to faulty perceptions about faith and God?

Truth 19

JESUS IS THE ULTIMATE CELEBRITY ENDORSER

*"Now when Jesus was born in Bethlehem of Judea in
the days of Herod the king, behold, wise men from
the East came to Jerusalem, saying, 'Where is he who
has been born king of the Jews? For we have seen his
star in the East, and have come to worship him.'"*
— MATTHEW 2:1–2

Secular companies love to promote their brands using
celebrity endorsers. Celebrities comes with star power;
they are known and often loved. For a brand, the hope is
that the passion that audiences have for a star will rub off
on the brand itself, captivating the imagination and driving
sales.

Alas, often celebrities cause significant problems for
a brand as well. If the celebrity does something wrong or
makes a mistake, that also reflects on the brand. The brand
world is littered with celebrities who caused enormous problems for the companies they represented. Names such as

O. J. Simpson for Hertz, Jared Fogle for Subway, and Michael Vick for Nike are just a few of the celebrity endorsers that backfired loudly and horribly for brands.

Or take another example. Lance Armstrong seemed to have the world on a string, when he fought off cancer, and then when he won the Tour de France multiple years in a row. Cyclist extraordinaire, he had multiple contracts to serve as a celebrity endorser for such big brands and organizations as Nike, Anheuser-Busch, Oakley, 24-hour Fitness, and more. Then news broke of the insurmountable evidence that he had used performance-enhancing drugs. Eight brands, all in one day, pulled their contracts with him. Why? Because his damaged image reflected poorly on their brands, so much so that they had to distance themselves from his endorsement immediately.

Many brands actually create characters primarily because they do not want to risk their brand with celebrities. Brand characters are easy to control and manage, and for a business, not nearly as risky as the current stars of the day.

For faith-based organizations, however, there is a built-in, original "star" in the person of Christ. Christ is the ultimate celebrity endorser. But of course, it's even better than that, because Jesus does not simply endorse our brand from the outside. He is the heart and life of our brand and mission. So for faith-based organizations, no other celebrity endorser is needed. There is one Christ who is well known, loved, and respected. The magi followed the star to find the King of the Jews, Jesus Christ. There is no other star needed to give our faith credibility. In fact, when we seek such stars, problems inevitably arise.

Often, famous pastors fall significantly when they become too popular in their own right: Jimmy Swaggart and Jim Bakker are just two examples. As pastors with a strong media presence, they served as "celebrity endorsers" for the churches they led. However, like all celebrity endorsers, they are human. They failed or made mistakes, thus hurting their churches and their flocks in the process. When organizations and parishes keep the focus on Christ, there is no risk of an additional celebrity damaging the church.

Dynamic Catholic does so much right when it comes to marketing. One especially outstanding effort is Matthew Kelly's book *Rediscover Jesus*. This work does two things: it focuses on Jesus, and it invites you to rediscover him. Dynamic Catholic recognizes that many people know Christ; they just have to become reacquainted or need to deepen their knowledge. In this way, Dynamic Catholic looks at Jesus as a celebrity. Even if you know him, trust him, and love him, they give you even more reasons to do so.

Consider your ministry, parish, or organization. What role does Christ play in your work? Can you invite people to a deeper experience because Christ is with you, in the midst of your work?

Much as the magi followed Christ's "star," people today want to follow him as well. With Jesus at the center of your organization, ministry, or parish, his light will shine on the work you are doing. At the same time, the work you do will bring those you serve closer to God. Just as the wise men saw Jesus' star and traveled to pay him homage, so Christ's star rises for you and those you serve as well. Share his star as you reach out and invite others to love and worship him.

FOR REFLECTION

What role does Jesus play in promoting and strengthening your brand? Do you keep him at the core of your mission and messaging?

What are some ways that you can help others to honor Jesus in a deeper way than they revere celebrity personalities (sports figures, actors, politicians)?

Truth 20

SATISFACTION COMES FROM BEING YOUR BEST

"All things are full of weariness; a man
cannot utter it; the eye is not satisfied with
seeing, nor the ear filled with hearing."
— ECCLESIASTES 1:8

Why is it that humans constantly seek more and more? As Ecclesiastes points out beautifully, "The eye is not satisfied with seeing, nor the ear filled with hearing." Being satisfied seems to be difficult not just for people, but for brands and organizations as well.

Some of the strongest, most memorable brands are those that have found their role in the marketplace. They have pursued excellence and have become known as the best in a category. Volvo was known for being the best in car safety, while BMW is known for driving performance. Brooks Brothers is known for distinguished men's suits, while the well-heeled woman turns to a brand like Chanel for classic clothes.

Those brands have built their reputations on being the best in a particular category. The challenge occurs when they are not satisfied — when they want more and more. In the commercial marketplace, that typically means more sales, more volume, more money. As a result of this desire to create more, a brand or business may reach beyond what it does well. Typically, this backfires, causing problems for the brand or business. Volvo started advertising its stylish lines, which just muddled its safety message. A reputation for being the best is built on doing the same thing well, year after year. When something new is brought into the mix, focus is lost and consumers get confused.

For years, Johnnette Benkovic Williams has been encouraging authentic femininity as she strives to transform the world, one woman at a time, through her Women of Grace ministry. I have been told about Women of Grace many times, often by men. Her messages resonate with them as well as women. However, she knows that her space is to help develop women of grace, and that continues to be her focus. This is what she does best, and she does not stray from it.

Lighthouse Catholic Media provides CDs and audio presentations for Catholics, with a special emphasis on information and insights for fallen-away Catholics. Staying focused on their message and the role that they play, especially in parishes, they have delivered millions of audio presentations to Catholics around the world. They are the best at delivering audio content that matters, and they do more of that each and every year.

When an organization starts to realize success, to see more followers, and to obtain more funding, it is easy to take advantage of the brand halo and try to offer new services or reach new target audiences. Be careful. Brand halos are created because the organization has developed an expertise and a reputation for being the best in a category. The easiest way to tarnish that halo is to venture out to other services or types of projects and take for granted what it required to become the best in that category.

When we are not satisfied by the work we do, or by the messages we share, things become cluttered. As a result, they become wearisome (as Ecclesiastes warns) for us as well as for our customers. If you are the best at something, be satisfied. Do not become wearisome to those you serve.

FOR REFLECTION

What is the one thing you are the best at doing?

How do you deal with feeling overwhelmed and burnout? What are some ways you can recharge?

Truth 21

GREAT POSITIONS ENDURE

"For the LORD *is good; his steadfast love endures for ever, and his faithfulness to all generations."*
— PSALM 100:5

To endure means both to remain in existence and to suffer. Brands and organizations must endure, especially when it comes to their position in the market. A brand's position describes the role it plays in the market. A great position will endure, regardless of societal changes.

The positioning of your brand is one of your most critical undertakings in marketing and communications. It sets the platform for your brand, conveying what makes you unique and why your organization or ministry should be preferred in the marketplace. It should be developed with an eye to longevity, something the brand can deliver on year after year. The position is the primary means by which you will connect your service or products with your customers or users. It provides the rationale as to why you are the right option for them. Once a strong position is developed, your organization must consistently deliver on that position.

Strong positions are enduring because they work despite the changes in the marketplace. Allstate Insurance uses the tagline "You're in good hands with Allstate," conveying a position of trust, comfort, and confidence. When Allstate developed that tagline back in the 1950s, they could not possibly have imagined the technology of today, the homes and cars that would be developed, the various ways that insurance would be needed. However, their position of trust, comfort, and confidence endures, even as society has changed and the items that they insure have evolved.

Catholic Charities has been serving those in need for more than one hundred years. The organization's work has shifted as society has changed. In the wake of Hurricanes Katrina and Rita, Catholic Charities launched an effort to cut poverty in half in the United States. That work addressed a newly discovered need; and yet it was completely consistent with the position of the organization.

On the other hand, Heinz forgot what their position in the market was all about when they introduced a green squirt ketchup. It was created initially as a promotion in support of the movie *Shrek*. In the beginning, kids enjoyed the idea of green ketchup that could be squirted out. But that didn't last long, as green ketchup didn't work with the Heinz tagline of "Grown Not Made," or the brand's position as fresh and preservative-free. The product flopped, and Heinz removed it from the market in 2006.

Both Allstate and Catholic Charities have strong positions because they have identified the universal need or problem that they address. Allstate positions their brand around a consumer's need to trust their insurance to handle every situation. Catholic Charities positions themselves around taking care of those in need. By centering on the problem that is addressed, they created positions that are long-lasting, that can endure. On the other hand, Heinz quickly realized when they stepped too far away from their position, and they corrected accordingly.

A position that endures will handle the challenges of societal changes, and it will be counted on for years to come. Your members, consumers, and users will trust you when you develop a brand position that endures for them.

FOR REFLECTION

How can you ensure that your role in society will last?

What are some practical ways you can strengthen your current position?

Truth 22

YOUR NAME IS THE CORNERSTONE OF YOUR BRAND

"A good name is to be chosen rather than great riches, and favor is better than silver or gold."
— PROVERBS 22:1

One element of your brand is utilized in absolutely everything you do, and that is your name. Your name is foundational to the perceptions created about your brand, your ministry, and your organization. Great names stand out and bring interest and understanding to your work.

The secular world is filled with outstanding names that have resonated with consumers for years. Names such as Irish Spring, Purina Puppy Chow, Jiffy Lube, and Close-Up Toothpaste all richly convey the essence of their brand. Irish Spring is the soap that leaves you fresh and clean, and Puppy Chow clearly identifies the niche or target for dog food. Jiffy Lube makes it clear that the oil change will be done quickly, while Close-Up gives you confidence that you can get close to a loved one with that toothpaste.

Names can also be more functional in nature. You know exactly what Build-A-Bear is just by the name. SHOWTIME obviously refers to movies. Some organizations prefer to create names and imbue the name with meaning and value. Monsanto created the Genuity brand for its biotechnology traits for corn, soybeans, cotton, and specialty crops, merging the words *genetics* and *unity*.

Some companies prefer to use random words as their names. Before Apple was known for computers, an apple was simply a piece of fruit. Creating names or using existing words can be very effective, but also very expensive. Money needs to be spent to not only introduce your product, but also to help consumers understand that this time around, *apple* means a computer and not a piece of fruit.

For faith-based organizations, names are equally critical. Faith-based organizations have a clear advantage in that often the names of saints or elements of faith can serve as the name of a mission or parish. When a well-known name is used, such as Saint Francis or Saint Joseph, it is critical that the essence of the saint be a part of the brand and messaging, or there will be a disconnect for the user. By way of an extreme example, if you created a ministry to assist people with computer technology, calling the ministry St. Francis Technology could be quite confusing, because Saint Francis is known for his work with the poor, the environment, and animals, not technology.

Many Catholic organizations are interested in creating a name that continues to fit as they expand and develop. A great example is Dynamic Catholic. The name clearly tells you the essence of the organization's brand and mission, which is to help enliven Catholics through their work. Likewise, Catholic Answers is an excellent example of a functional name. From that name you clearly know that you will receive answers to Catholic questions. Another great name out there is Catholic Mom, an organization providing wonderful Catholic resources to — you guessed it — Catholic mothers.

Everything you communicate about your brand, mission, ministry, or parish starts with your name. The brand name will carry the message of your organization for years to come, so spending time identifying the right name is time well spent. It is the mental hook for your customers that will connect them to the values you provide, the promise you make, and the services you offer. Your name is the cornerstone of your brand; and, as conveyed in Proverbs 22:1, a good name is more desirable than great riches.

FOR REFLECTION

How does your brand's name reflect and express your core message?

How did you choose your brand's name? What do you hope it communicates?

Truth 23

YOUR BRAND DRIVES YOUR ORGANIZATION'S CULTURE

"While you have the light, believe in the light,
that you may become sons of light."
— JOHN 12:36

One of the most important aspects of building a strong organizational culture is building a strong brand. A brand is your promise — what you do and why your organization, parish, or ministry can be trusted. Customers, consumers, and users need to know this, but so do your employees, staff, and volunteers.

Brands often serve as the light for an organization, provided they are well articulated. The promise of the brand, the position and messaging, help bring clarity to an organization and its staff. Organizations can rally around and understand brands because they convey intentionality and purpose.

Organizations usually try to build positive cultures for their employees. Those cultures are much easier to develop when there is clarity around the brand. Consider Disney. As a brand, we know that Disneyland promises to be the "happiest place on earth." An organization such as Disney could not possibly deliver happiness to its customers if the employees and staff did not understand and, in fact, experience that happiness as well. Disney understands what the brand means to external audiences and lives it internally as well, and that shapes its culture.

Large corporations often get into trouble with culture after they have purchased other brands and businesses. Ingersoll Rand is a great example. A large business with a solid culture in its own right, it purchased the HVAC giant Trane. The addition of Trane doubled the size of Ingersoll Rand, but it also created a new corporate entity with two different cultures. Employees of this new entity struggled to understand what the culture really was. The Trane brand was exceptionally strong, and employees passionately supported it, lived the brand, and had a culture reflective of the brand. Because of the acquisition, Trane was now simply a part of the whole, and the brand no longer set the culture and direction of the entire organization. It took years of work with the brands and the employees before a clear culture emerged that embodied elements from both Trane and Ingersoll Rand.

Consider a Catholic example. Ave Maria University is a Catholic school in southwest Florida. This Catholic liberal arts school was inspired by Saint John Paul II and Saint Teresa of Calcutta. The university started in 2003 with a clear mission: to provide excellent education in a faith-rich environment. Since its founding, both the school and the town of Ave Maria have continued to grow. The Catholic roots are obvious, with street names like Roma Street and Assisi Avenue, and the Ave Maria parish in the center of town. However, it is the culture that really captures attention. People go out of their way to help out a stranger, to share little nuggets about the town (places to see or things to do). Everyone you meet exudes gratitude and joy. That type of culture does not happen by accident. A commitment to living the Catholic faith, the core of their brand, is what causes Ave Maria and the surrounding town to have such a clear culture.

Remember, the brand should be the light for your organization. It highlights the promise and the values you hold dear. As you believe in the light, you strengthen your organization's commitment to the brand, and your carry the message forward, building a vibrant culture.

FOR REFLECTION

What are your core values, and how do they connect to your daily life and work?

What are some of the ways you have created a positive culture around your faith and spiritual activities?

Truth 24

CONSISTENCY IS INTENTIONAL AND CRITICAL IN MARKETING

*"But when they had fed to the full,
they were filled, and their heart was
lifted up; therefore they forgot me."*
— Hosea 13:6

There is a big difference between consistency and complacency. Consistency is intentional; it takes focused work. Complacency, on the other hand, is the exact opposite: it is lack of focus, performing or doing work without intention. While the meanings are quite different, it is very easy for those two approaches to be conflated and confused. From a marketing perspective, that can be disastrous.

Blockbuster Video is a classic example of complacency. Blockbuster owned the market in video rentals. People would spend a great deal of time searching their stores for the perfect video to watch. In the early 2000s, Blockbuster had more than nine thousand stores worldwide. By 2010, they were filing for bankruptcy, and by 2013, the last of the company-owned stores were closed. Blockbuster was complacent as new technologies such as Netflix, Redbox, and streaming on-demand were released. Surely, consumers would not leave the Blockbuster stores they loved. A few short years later, the results of their complacency in the market were critically apparent.

Consistency is a critical component of brand success. Consistency speaks to being intentional in every aspect of the brand. The look of the brand — for instance, how the logo is used, the colors of the marketing materials, the fonts and typefaces — must be considered carefully and used consistently. But these are simple examples. Consistency must occur throughout all dimensions of the brand, including the messaging, the experience, and the product or service itself.

The sad example of complacency in the Catholic Church right now is the sex abuse crisis. The abuse being identified is horrific. Many of those in leadership in the Church exhibited complacency in the face of allegations of abuse, and the results have been deeply distressing, to say the least. We are witnessing great sadness in the Church today in large part because of this complacency, which led leadership to fail to hold accountable the perpetrators of the abuse.

Complacency can exist anywhere and everywhere, however, not just in leadership. Evidence of complacency abounds in society, including our parishes and ministries. For instance, when you start to notice the same people missing from Mass each Sunday, do you call and check on them? Do you have the same leaders for every parish ministry, because they are the only ones who say yes when no one else will step up? If you are in a conversation with someone about the Catholic faith and they are challenging you, do you take on the conversation or change the topic? When it comes to our faith, each Christian has to push back against complacency in the Church and in our own minds and hearts.

From a marketing perspective, complacency can take many forms. It can be failing to send out a thank you note in a timely way after a donation. It can be use of an old logo, not taking the extra minute to make sure the logo is current and colors correct. It can be slow updates to a website.

Complacency is easy. It is easy to turn a blind eye and look away from a problem. It is much harder to be consistent: to know right from wrong and to act on it accordingly. Complacency occurs, as is pointed out in Hosea 13:6, when one is satisfied. When a brand, organization, or entity is satisfied, it also becomes proud. It suspects that it can ride on its brand awareness, presence, and knowledge. The greatest vigilance is required when a brand has a strong reputation, for that is when it's easiest to be complacent.

From a marketing perspective, complacency manifests as not worrying about the language or messaging of a brochure, posting all sorts of things on social media, or offering events that do not completely align with the mission but are still "good things to do."

Consistency requires intentionality. It requires knowing exactly what you are about, what your brand promise is, what experience you are providing, what messages you want to communicate, and the look and feel that you will use when communicating those messages. It is holding each activity up to the mirror and asking whether it is true to the brand of your organization, ministry, mission, or parish.

Do not be satisfied; do not become proud; do not forget; do not be complacent. Rather, be intentional; be true; be consistent. This is critical.

FOR REFLECTION

What steps can you take to combat complacency in your faith?

How can you help those around you to be excited about their faith and engaged in their parish?

Truth 25

CONSUMERS WILL NOT BUY IF YOU AREN'T DIFFERENT

"The prophets who prophesied of the grace that was to be yours searched and inquired about this salvation."
1 PETER 1:10

A s Christians, we are called to serve others with the very grace God has given us. God reminds us that each of us has value and certain gifts that make us truly distinct. He wants us to share our talents, remembering that we are part of the whole. This is also true with brands, especially when it comes to faith-based organizations, ministries, and parishes: God gave you your gifts. So be yourself and stand out.

In the world today, people are bombarded with brands, messages, and products. As we mentioned in Truth 3, the average person sees more than five thousand marketing messages a day, and this does not include everything on social media.

If people are so bombarded with messaging, how can your message ever stand out? Often, organizations just try to copy what others are doing. If it works for someone else, perhaps it will work for us, they think. While imitation is a sincere form of flattery, it does not work for marketing. If we want someone to choose us (buy our book, listen to our speech, come to our convention, attend our parish), we need to stand out.

If we want people to choose us, we must be different. We must promise something that does not already exist. This requires digging deep into your brand and what it offers, understanding what you really provide. It is not just a book, a speech, or a parish. It is a message, an element of uniting with God that cannot be found elsewhere.

Granted, we all use similar tools for sharing our brand. We may present the message in a book, we may use social media, or we may even place an advertisement. But the brand itself must be different. It must cause someone to take notice. It must cause someone to remember it. It must be compelling, and it must encourage action. When brands do that in a unique way, they get chosen.

You may remember Zune, introduced by Microsoft in 2006 to compete with Apple's very popular iPod. By 2012, it was discontinued as Microsoft tried to recover from significant sales declines attributed to Zune. Zune had lots of issues, including bugs that caused performance problems. However, the bigger issue may very well have been that it was simply a "me-too" product. It wasn't all that different from Apple's iPod, and it was late to the party, so why would anyone need it?

Often, we are afraid to be different. We want to fit in with the crowd. As marketers, we are afraid to be different, because we are afraid we will fail. Yet our differences and uniqueness are what matter most for our success.

Find your gift. Find your brand's gift and proclaim it loudly. Don't copy someone else's gift or try to imitate what another brand is doing. Do your thing and do it well. Don't be afraid to be different. If you were not different, why would anyone choose you?

FOR REFLECTION

What qualities and skills make your organization or mission stand out?

How have you overcome the struggle to compare yourself to others who seem more gifted or more successful?

Truth 26

THE BEST TAGLINES ARE MEANINGFUL, MEMORABLE, AND MOTIVATING

"What then shall we say to this?
If God is for us, who is against us?"
— Romans 8:31

In today's fast-paced society, people love taglines — the pithy little phrases that capture the essence of brands. The best taglines grow so ingrained that they become part of our vernacular, like "Just do it" or "Keeps going and going and going" or "Can you hear me now?"

Could Romans 8:31 be a tagline for building the kingdom of God on earth? Perhaps it could. In its simplicity, it strikes a chord that any person can clearly understand. It embodies the most critical elements of effective taglines: it is meaningful, memorable, and motivating.

The most effective taglines in marketing have these three critical components, which I call the Three Ms of Taglines. Let's explore each of these in detail, using the example of a tagline from a faith community that has gotten it right. Dynamic Catholic's tagline is Be bold. Be Catholic.

It is critical to remember that a tagline has to be considered in the context of the consumer, the person you are talking to in the market. So a meaningful tagline needs to be meaningful to the person you are trying to attract. It doesn't really matter if it is meaningful to your team, as your team is already committed. But what about your target audience, those you would like to welcome to your organization, convention, or parish? Will they care about it?

Dynamic Catholic's tagline is meaningful in a few ways. Many people are quietly Catholic, but they are certainly not bold about it. Dynamic Catholic is challenging that with the materials they share and the work they do, and their tagline states that beautifully. They view their role as encouraging and equipping Catholics to share their faith boldly. As a result, their tagline is meaningful in that it communicates their promise.

The second important part of a tagline is that people need to be able to remember it easily. When they are short and sweet, when they are clever, when they roll off the tongue easily, that is when taglines tend to be memorable. Alliteration or other mnemonic devices can be useful in making a phrase stand out for people.

Having a memorable tagline is important because we want it to stick with people. We want them to easily recall it when necessary. With enough spending, corporations can make even taglines that are not clever or memorable stick with audiences through sheer force. Faith-based organizations, however, typically don't have the budgets to drive broad communication of a tagline. So for those of us working to spread God's kingdom, it is critical that we focus on developing a memorable tagline.

Dynamic Catholic's tagline is quite memorable: Be bold. Be Catholic. It is simple and clever, but it is also intentional. Notice how the only word that doesn't start with a "b" is *Catholic*. This causes Catholic to stand out, which is exactly what they want to help Catholics do.

The third important element of a tagline is that it is motivating. This means that it causes or inspires a consumer to do something, to take some type of action. A meaningful and memorable tagline that does not lead to action will fall on its face. Think back to Nike's tagline, "Just do it." An important part of its strength is its motivating nature. You feel encouraged that you can do it, too. It works for everyone, regardless of what you are trying to do.

When it comes to motivation, Dynamic Catholic's tagline once again gets it right. Beyond being meaningful and memorable, this tagline is quite motivating. It inspires action; it encourages you to live your faith out loud.

Let's look again at Saint Paul's words in his letter to the Romans: "If God is for us, who can be against us?" It is meaningful as, of course, we want to stand with God. It is memorable in its simplicity. It is motivating to know that we have God on our side. Of course, no Bible verse was written to be a tagline. Yet, many verses of Scripture do resonate with us so deeply because they are so meaningful, memorable, and motivating. Let the Lord's word inspire you as you craft the tagline that is meaningful, memorable, and motivating for your organization.

FOR REFLECTION

Do you have a tagline? If so, describe how it is meaningful, memorable, and motivating.

If you don't have a tagline, come up with one or two possibilities (making sure they are meaningful, memorable, and motivating).

Truth 27

CUSTOMER SERVICE IS THE TOUCHPOINT OF YOUR BRAND

"Through love be servants of one another."
— GALATIANS 5:13

Every interaction that your consumer or customer has with your brand is considered a touchpoint. In this day and age, there are millions of touchpoints for each brand, from social media interactions, to advertisements, to packaging, to customer service. Yet the most meaningful touchpoints are those in service of your customer, and often the littlest interactions have the biggest impact.

Consider your faith-based organization. How do you interact with people? Are you present to them and their needs, or do you shuffle them through as another item on your to-do list? How do you answer the phone? How do you welcome people to your organization? How do you handle a financial contribution? Every little interaction conveys to them how you value them as a parishioner, a member, a volunteer, or, perhaps, a partner.

Some organizations are simply brilliant in their interactions with customers and consumers. It should come as no surprise that consumers love them right back. Disney is a great example. Disney World strives to be the "most magical place on earth," and its employees are trained to create magical moments at every turn. That happens in large part because they evaluate the processes for their guests, which allows them to improve each and every step. For instance, keeping track of where a guest parks in the morning allows them to help get the guest right to their car at night.

True, Disney uses lots of technology in service of the customer. Technology can help shorten ride lines or keep the sound consistent throughout the park. But more than that, the company does not assign just a few people to customer service; rather, everyone is part of the customer experience. Disney understands that interactions occur in all sorts of ways, and each one can serve as a touchpoint for the brand.

Now let's consider a faith-based organization that does this well. Have you ever visited a Pauline Books and Media store? Run by the Daughters of St. Paul, these stores are such a treat. When customers walk in, a sister is sure to welcome them and ask whether they are looking for anything in particular. The music is soft and inspirational. There is a reading corner, if you want to stay and thumb through something. Of course, there is a place for children to read and play. It is not uncommon to hear someone confide in a sister about a family member, a faith experience, or an illness; this bookstore is a safe place for those discussions. Each touchpoint helps to create a faith-filled experience when a customer visits a Pauline store.

Think about your organization and consider your customer service. What are the touchpoints you can provide? Recall Our Lord's words in the Gospel: "Through love be servants of one another." What does it look like for you to walk one mile with your customer? How do you serve with love? You are there to serve, serve well, and serve further as you lead your customers to God.

FOR REFLECTION

How do you welcome new people to your organization or to your parish? What steps do you take to make sure they feel valued and respected?

Make a list of three new touchpoints you might add to make your customer's experience even richer.

Truth 28

MARKETING AND EVANGELIZATION ARE CONNECTED, BUT DISTINCT

"He said to them, 'Cast the net on the right side of the boat, and you will find some.' So they cast it, and now they were not able to haul it in, for the quantity of fish."
— JOHN 21:6

Marketing and evangelization are distinct functions with different purposes. Yet each is vitally important for a faith-based organization, ministry, or parish.

How are marketing and evangelization different? Marketing is about casting a wide net. It helps you know where to place the net, on which side of the boat. From a marketing perspective, that means putting your message and your brand out to many people as effectively as possible. It means knowing your audience and their needs. Evangelization is about reaching people at the personal level, engaging in relationship with them and sharing with them, in an effort to draw them closer to God.

When it comes to using marketing tools to help build God's kingdom, it can be helpful to compare marketing and evangelization to marketing and sales in the corporate world. Please hear me out! Marketing in the corporate sphere is designed to create awareness, to help people understand that the product or service is available. Marketing "greases the wheel," so to speak, in an effort to make it easier for sales to enter into a meaningful discussion.

Awareness is simply a measurement of whether a consumer knows of you. Study after study shows consumers will never make a purchase if they do not know who or what you are, so marketing is the critical first step. As awareness grows, it becomes easier for a salesperson to make the case for the product or service. It becomes easier because people are more willing to listen, engage, and learn about the product or service.

Unfortunately, we as discussed earlier, marketing is often considered a bad word among Catholics. It is interesting to note that evangelization was also lost for a while. Pope Saint John Paul II introduced the New Evangelization, which has begun to reinvigorate the Church in our day. Thanks in large part to his teaching, and to the continuation of that work under Pope Benedict XVI and Pope Francis, we now see many different faith-based entities popping up to assist with Catholic evangelization throughout the world.

Yet consider the parallel to corporate sales and marketing. If our marketing is subpar, we make the job of evangelization incredibly difficult. We must build a Catholic brand that resonates for a broader audience in order to create awareness and open doors for the evangelizers to do their important work. This means that marketing, far from being a bad word, can make a great difference for our faith.

The most effective corporate marketers know that they must walk hand-in-hand with a sales organization. One without the other is rarely successful. In the same way, our marketing efforts for our faith-based organization, ministry, or parish must be placed in the service of evangelization.

FOR REFLECTION

Describe in your own words the difference between marketing and evangelization. How are they alike? How are they different?

How would you define the Catholic brand? How would someone in your neighborhood define it?

Truth 29

IT IS EASIER TO HIT A SMALLER TARGET

"I have not come to call the righteous,
but sinners to repentance."
— Luke 5:32

Christ provides a targeted, precise definition of the people he came to call, and this definition brings a great deal of clarity. His precision does not mean this is a small group of people. In fact, we know as Christians that he means all people. In fact, we know as Christians that he means all people. His precision here means that each of us can clearly know that he is speaking to us.

In marketing, it's tempting to answer the question, "Who are you trying to reach?" with, "Well, everyone!" Especially when it comes to our faith; we know that everyone needs God. While it is very true that everyone needs God, "everyone" is not who you are trying to reach. As an individual organization, it is important to look to Jesus as your role model: clearly define your audience. Remember that you only have a piece of the pie. You don't have to do it all; and, in fact, you can't.

Think about archery. In archery, you are aiming to hit a very small target, but the only goal is to hit the target. When we speak of a target in marketing, we mean something different. Unlike archery, marketing is not simply aiming to hit the target. It is also important to connect with the target audience, to share messages with them, and cause them to become loyal to you. In faith-based marketing, this might also require causing them to change something they are currently doing. That is a lot to ask. This is why it's critical to be exceptionally focused on your precise target. This means you are in a better position not only to "hit" them, but also to get your message to take root.

One way of thinking about defining your audience is recalling that your brand, your promise, is not for everyone. I know that you want it to be, but recall the farmer analogy from earlier: if this is the year that your farmer wants to plant corn, no amount of communication on soybeans will matter. It is just not his or her year to farm soybeans. The same is true for your work in faith. If someone is looking for faith information focused on children, no amount of marketing regarding senior citizens and God will be relevant. Your ministry simply is not for them at this time.

It is good to be really focused. I would even say it is critical. When you are focused, you are attractive to the specific group of people that is looking for what you have. To those people searching for you, you have value. You will not just reach them, but they will take notice of you, they will listen to you, and they may donate to you.

When I speak with organizations about being focused on their target audience, they become fearful. They don't want to miss out on sales or donations. They are afraid that their pie will become smaller as a result. In fact, the complete opposite happens. When you are focused, your audience understands what you are providing and they become committed. They become raving fans, and they share what you are doing with others who are then more likely to also become committed to your brand.

There is a big trend in the corporate world to pay influencers. Influencers are people on social media with followings of one thousand to one hundred thousand. These influencers are paid to share their love of a particular product with their followers. Why? Because their followers are intensely loyal and are more likely to purchase a product that the influencer suggests.

Think about that: enormous corporate entities are paying small influencers for access to their audiences. They want their message to reach those who care about it, who will do something with it. How much more important is this for you, since your message is so much more important?

So be specific in defining your target audience. It should include demographics and geography, as well as psychographics. What are the audience's values, attitudes, beliefs, lifestyles? In marketing for faith-based organizations, we also should consider whether they are new to faith or raised in it. Did they have a trigger, a conversion? Are they seekers, looking for information, or are they beginning to contribute to the faith dialogue? Understanding these motivations can help to ensure that you are defining your audience properly so your message will have the most impact.

FOR REFLECTION

Who is your target audience?

What motivates this audience, and how can you tailor your message to reach them?

Truth 30

BRAND EXTENSIONS OFTEN DIMINISH BRAND GROWTH

*"I am the true vine, and my Father is the
vinedresser. Every branch of mine that bears no fruit,
he takes away, and every branch that does bear fruit
he prunes, that it may bear more fruit."*
— JOHN 15:1–2

In the corporate world, the challenge is to grow, grow, grow.
In other words, the goal is to make more money. Knowing this, organizations often take a brand that is doing well and try to do more with it. Creating these new products or services under the umbrella of an existing brand is known as developing brand extensions. The brand is extended into a new space for the consumer with hopes that the extension will "bear fruit" for the company. While this can seem like the right way to grow, all too often, such extensions fall flat.

Brands, as we know, own a place in a consumer's mind.

The consumer understands what the brand is, when to use it, and why it matters. Creating brand extensions can be dangerous, because often, the consumer views the brand in a precise way, and adding extensions that are inconsistent with the consumer's view creates confusion.

An interesting extension came from Arizona Tea, who thought consumers would want a nice salty snack to go with their iced tea. They introduced Arizona Nachos Cheese Snack Tray, and it failed miserably. Consumers could not wrap their heads around a tea company providing nacho snacks. A similar fail occurred when Dr. Pepper tried to introduce Dr. Pepper BBQ sauce. This was another major brand flop, as consumers did not understand that extension. Cheetos likewise tried a brand extension by creating Cheetos-flavored lip balm. It never caught on.

Brand extensions can work, of course, but only when they are close to the original brand promise. Let's consider a Catholic example. Camp Wojtyla is an outdoor adventure camp located in the heart of the Colorado Rockies. Its founders believe in a God of adventure, one with a story and plan for everyone. They invite young people to enter into adventure with God. They have developed brand extensions that make sense because they are close to the camp's brand. The extensions include programs for different ages, as well as different types of adventure programs. This type of brand extension works because, as they extend out, people notice and understand. The extension makes sense, given their brand promise.

Many Catholic authors also do a good job of extending their brands in ways that make sense. (The various books that an author writes can be viewed as brand extensions for the author.) Scott Hahn is a popular and prolific author, with particular expertise in Scripture. He has written many books in this area, and he is highly regarded. Peter Kreeft is another prolific author, with at least seventy-five books penned. As a philosophy professor, he focuses on faith, often with a philosophical bent. These authors have both done well, though in very different spaces, primarily because they stay true to their brands. They may have multiple books, but those books are extensions that are consistent with their brand. They do not extend beyond what is plausible for their readers.

Be careful that your brand doesn't extend in directions that confuse your customers. Remember, brand extensions can often diminish growth and need to be pruned back to allow the branches that bear fruit the room to grow.

FOR REFLECTION

When it comes to God and issues of faith, what types of confusion in the minds of others have you encountered? What can you do to alleviate this?

What ways have you attempted to extend your brand into new areas? Was this successful? Why or why not?

Truth 31

REPOSITIONING IS OFTEN A FOOL'S CHASE

"The wisdom of a prudent man
is to discern his way, but the
folly of fools is deceiving."
— PROVERBS 14:8

In the marketing world, repositioning is taking a brand and shifting its meaning. It is virtually impossible to accomplish this, because the brand lives in the user's mind. Getting people to change their perception of your brand does not work, because they don't understand or even care about the brand nearly as much as you do.

Companies often pressure brand teams to reposition a brand in the search for greater loyalty and stronger sales; but unfortunately, repositioning is typically a fool's chase. There could be many reasons for companies to want to reposition their brands. Trends may change, and the company feels the need to reposition to keep up. Or perhaps the brand has never been clearly managed, so new people on the brand team think that they are the ones who can finally "get it right." The truth is, if a brand chases every trend, it will never stand proudly for what it delivers well. Likewise, if a brand changes at the whim of every brand manager, it will never stand tall in the marketplace.

Do you remember the brand Radio Shack? With declining sales, they tried to rebrand themselves as "The Shack," which was a dismal failure. Radio Shack for years had been a traditional store with small component parts for the hobbyist. As sales declined, they tried to shift to keep up with the evolving hip and cool technology market. To do so, they changed the name to The Shack and focused on selling mobile products at the expense of their core business. It did not take long before they had to close all their retail stores. Given the decline in retail and the energy in technology, could they have survived the changing market dynamics? While we will never be sure, we do know that trying to reposition a more traditional hobby company as a hip and cool technology firm failed miserably.

Did you ever have a conversation with someone who attended Catholic schools? If so, did they share examples of the nuns who were teachers slapping the hands of students with a ruler or measuring how long girls' uniform skirts were? If so, you are experiencing firsthand the challenge with repositioning. Even if nuns do not do these things today, or perhaps never did, there is a position in the minds of many regarding how nuns treated students.

Of course, the idea of strict nuns led to all sorts of stories, including the Broadway show *Nunsense* and its spinoffs. Part of its appeal is that while many people who went to Catholic school did not experience that type of behavior from sisters, they believe they were the lucky ones. This sense about sisters in education is a position that is very difficult to shake.

Why? Because it lives in the minds of people, regardless of the fabulous Catholic religious women teaching today.

Repositioning in marketing is often a fool's chase, for it requires you to change the minds of people. Positions are critical when they are first developed because, as we can see, changing the mind of a collective group of people is difficult, if not impossible. So starting with a clear position eliminates the need for potential marketing repositioning later on.

To be clear, when we talk about repositioning, that is strictly from a marketing perspective. Whatever work you do in or for the Church, your role is to introduce God, the Gospel, and our faith to others. Understanding your position in this important work will assist others as they discern their way to the Lord. God will do the heavy lifting of changing hearts; your role is to help get them to God.

For Reflection

What ways did Jesus use to change people's minds and hearts?

How might you employ something similar to reposition the way people think about faith, the Church, being Catholic?

Truth 32

CONSISTENCY BUILDS; COMPROMISE DESTROYS

*"'And you shall love the Lord your God with all
your heart, and with all your soul, and with all your
mind, and with all your strength.' The second is this,
'You shall love your neighbor as yourself.'"*
— MARK 12:30–31

This message that Christ brought us is so simple, isn't it?
But we all know it is certainly not easy. We want to love
everyone, and then someone cuts us off in traffic, or a store-
keeper is rude, or any numbers of other things in a given
day make it difficult to truly love everyone. But there is no
compromise in God's message: we must love everyone.

Effective brands do not allow for compromise, either.
Brands are built on consistency. Consistency of look and
feel, consistency of message, consistency of product, of service ... the list goes on. The reason is really quite simple:

Consumers do not know our brands nearly as well as we do. If we want to build loyalty with them, we must keep consumers in the forefront of our minds and realize that the slightest change may confuse them.

Compromise is an intentional shift away from the consistency directed by the brand. In Truth 24 we talked about complacency, which is not intentional but rather a lack of thought or caring enough to keep the brand consistent. Compromise speaks to a willingness to change, usually in order to keep everyone in an organization happy. However, while compromise perhaps can help individuals feel good, it will not benefit your brand or your marketing.

The world of corporate brand marketing is very rigorous. Colors must be exactly right; visuals are defined and must be used only in approved manners. Creative briefs outline everything from the role of the brand to the tone of every communication. On top of this, in the corporate world there are teams of people watching, measuring, and tweaking the brand to keep it on track.

They do this because they know that the slightest compromise can begin to erode their brand. Compromising in pricing is often a common thing that brands have to address. It is tempting to price a brand or a product just below a competitor with hopes of generating more sales. However, the opposite often occurs, and price compromise causes some people to question why that brand is lower. They wonder whether there is something wrong with the product or brand. Compromise in a brand, even if it seems small, causes confusion. Consumers don't know your brand as well, so even little things can change their perceptions of you, which is not what you want.

Compromise is a slippery slope. In the spirit of trying to keep everyone happy, it is far too easy to allow everyone to have a say, or to cave to pressure from other departments, and this creates disconnects for your customer. While compromise can be helpful in running an organization, it is not helpful in trying to attract followers. Furthermore, it sets the stage for additional compromise. If it is okay to shift from light blue to sky blue, then is a shift from pink to purple that far behind?

For your brand to stand strong, it must be clear and consistent. Why? In large part because consumers are not nearly as familiar with your brand as you are, and they are bombarded with thousands of messages a day. Your message can so easily get lost in the deluge. If you can craft a consistent brand with consistent messaging, those you are trying to reach are more likely to see it and recognize it as something they want or need.

In the corporate world, brand managers are often seen as "brand police," literally approving and suggesting revisions for every item that leaves the company's doors. Most often, brand teams develop "brand books" — brand guidelines that highlight the logo and how it can be used, the color palettes that are available for use, the core messaging statements, and other elements that need to remain consistent for the brand. This is also a very helpful approach for a faith-centered organization. Even if you have just a few people, providing a tool that helps everyone consistently know, use, and share your brand will not only help the others on your team, but will minimize the need for any compromise along the way.

The opportunity to compromise is present in many different ways in an organization, from the colors of the brand, to the logo used, to the key messages. But even more fundamentally, compromise can occur in how you treat people and whether you consistently deliver what you promise. All of these pieces can be defined, and they should be defined.

Once they are defined, you can focus on delivering them consistently, appropriately, without compromise.

The very simple message that Christ shared was to love God with all you have and to love your neighbor as yourself. That message clearly leaves no room for compromise. It is so simple, though not necessarily easy. The same is true with your brand: keep it true, and don't compromise. That is very simple to do as well; and again, it's not very easy.

FOR REFLECTION

Where have you been tempted to cut corners and compromise an aspect of your work? If you gave in to the temptation, what was the result?

What elements of your brand are you careful not to compromise?

Truth 33

CLEAR IS MORE CRITICAL THAN CLEVER

*"For we did not follow cleverly devised
myths when we made known to you
the power and coming of our Lord Jesus Christ,
but we were eyewitnesses of his majesty."*
— 2 PETER 1:16

Marketers and communicators can be quite creative. While there is real benefit to creativity, the focus should always be on the message and not on how cleverly the story can be told. Don't get so caught up in doing fabulously creative marketing that you miss the point: that your role is to convey your message to your market. The verse above from Peter's second letter is pointed: you do not want people to follow "cleverly devised myths." Being too clever can result in just that. It can take you from a point of clarity and insight to the point where people no longer believe you.

The Pets.com sock puppet from a few years ago is such a classic example of this. Yes, a dog sock puppet was clever and captured attention. That dog sock puppet showed up all over the place. The problem was that while it was clever, it did not convey an effective message about Pets.com. Before too long, the company was selling the sock puppet, but sales of its mainline products — pet supplies — were dwindling. If you Google it now, the headlines tell you the story: "Pets.com killed by sock puppet," says MarketWatch. The sock puppet was clever, but it did not convey the real offer or message of the company.

A cleverly conveyed message that worked well was the very simple "Got milk" campaign. This campaign featured milk mustaches on all sorts of different people, celebrities included. More than clever, it enhanced the message, bringing attention to the idea of drinking more milk.

We don't want the clever to overshadow the message, but having some cleverness or pizzazz in your marketing or communication is not a bad thing. On the contrary, it can be very effective. It can stimulate interest, be memorable, and create enthusiasm for your brand.

Many brands utilize characters as a way of conveying their message. Characters such as Tony the Tiger or the AFLAC Duck have the latitude to do some interesting — and yes, clever — things to bring attention to the product, service, or message. Even still, those brand managers are spending countless hours ensuring that their characters do not overshadow their brand.

When I managed the Energizer brand some years ago, not being overly clever with the bunny was core to the work I did. Time after time, promotion agencies would come in all excited about the things they could do with the "bunny." However, the bunny was a device. Our business was batteries, which had to be our message.

A Catholic radio show I particularly like is *Driving*

Home the Faith, on Sacred Heart Radio in Cincinnati. Fr. Rob Jack hosts the show every afternoon, during Cincinnati's rush-hour traffic. A clever title, it also packs a strong punch. The topics he covers address various aspects of faith, so the show truly does drive home the Faith. It is not a "cleverly devised myth," but rather truly provides "eyewitnesses" to deepening faith.

Being too clever can take you to a place of devised myth, which will not convey the message of your service, mission, or organization. Rather, remember that your role is to make "eyewitnesses" to your market. You want people to know who you are and what you do. Being clever can highlight who and what you are, but it should never overshadow it.

FOR REFLECTION

How have you cleverly designed your message (your website, your branding) to reach people in compelling ways?

In your own messaging, what are some ways of being too clever that you should avoid?

Truth 34

MANAGING BRANDS IS OFTEN THE OPPOSITE OF COMMON SENSE

"O simple ones, learn prudence;
O foolish men, pay attention."
— PROVERBS 8:5

So many times, I hear young marketers claim that marketing is simply common sense. Those of us seasoned in marketing shake our heads, for nothing could be further from the truth. Common sense implies that if it works for you, it works for everyone. Common sense suggests that education, marketing theory, and strategy are not necessary. Common sense comes from the mind of each individual, and that is where the problem exists.

As a society, we live with marketing. It is on our TVs, our phones, our cars, our computers, our billboards. We are bombarded by messages all day long. Naturally, people are motivated by some messages and turned off by others, and this is different for all of us. Because people live with marketing, they suspect that what they love is right and great. In fact, they love a particular message because, somewhere, a marketer understands their behavior, their sensibilities, and what matters to them. That is not common sense; that is thoughtful marketing.

Now, lest you be concerned that this is not in keeping with your faith-based work, rest assured: thoughtful marketing is not manipulative marketing. (Sadly, the few manipulative marketers give everyone a bad name.) Consider marketing to be a conversation you are having with someone. In an effective conversation, you think about the individual, what matters to them, how to share an insight with them effectively. You are thinking about them first and foremost. Marketing is the same type of exercise.

Marketing, when done well, is quite strategic. It is based on insights regarding a precise target audience. It considers the promise of the brand, the abilities of a company to deliver on the promise, and the tools and techniques most impactful for motivating customers to choose the brand.

All too often, organizations promote people who are good communicators or good with people to brand and marketing roles. Unfortunately, they may be great people, but in the absence of a strong understanding of marketing strategies, they rely on their own common sense. Believe it or not, that can be detrimental to the brand, the marketing, and the organization.

One company used to give marketing positions to their outstanding sales representatives. It was a feather in a salesperson's cap to be "promoted" to marketing for a stint. After a few years of this, the company couldn't understand why sales were lacking and customers no longer loved the brand. A deep dive into the marketing side of the business yielded a few interesting insights. Most of the marketing activities were deep discounts and promotional efforts. While a favorite of sales organizations, these do not create deep loyalty with customers. The salespeople in marketing did what was common sense to them: they offered promotions and discounts. Because those are short-term efforts and do not speak to sustainable loyalty, customers were leaving the brand for other options.

Catholic Answers is a great example of a faith-based organization that does not rely solely on common sense for marketing. Their entire premise is to arm Catholics with the knowledge they need to defend the Faith and answer critics. Their marketing is intentional and insightful, as they know their audience and the information their audience needs to defend Catholicism. Catholic Answers completely understands that the common sense of an individual Catholic is not the same as deep knowledge of and education on a topic — in this case, our faith.

Marketing is all about spending time understanding what matters to others and recognizing that, while you may like one thing, someone else appreciates another. Marketing is the opposite of common sense. In marketing it can actually be naïve to rely on common sense. Instead, gain a deep sense of your consumers and users, so that your marketing can speak effectively to your audiences.

FOR REFLECTION

How can you be strategic in your marketing efforts without being manipulative?

Especially for faith-based enterprises, how can you make sure your marketing efforts are practical and authentic?

Truth 35

NOTHING HAPPENS UNTIL YOU ARE AVAILABLE

"And I heard the voice of the Lord saying,
'Whom shall I send, and who will go for us?'
Then I said, 'Here am I! Send me.'"
— Isaiah 6:8

Nothing happens until your products or your services are available. This fact seems so simple, yet it is often over-looked. True, you can market in anticipation of a new launch or a grand opening. However, the basis of any brand promise is performance, or doing what you say you are going to do. This means your product or service must actually be available.

In the marketing world, there are lots of models that describe how marketing works and can be most effective. One of the most basic purchase decision models is a ladder, which shows how any person makes a decision to purchase and ultimately becomes loyal to a brand. At the very base of that

ladder is availability. If your product or service is not available, there is no way you can get groups of people to purchase,
fund, or support you.

What does this mean for all the great ideas out there? A
great idea is simply that: an idea. For someone to participate
in your ministry, attend your parish, or support your mission,
you must have your services developed or your products created and available for sale. Again, it is a simple idea, but so
critical.

Too many times, people get ahead of the game and start
marketing well before they have the idea fleshed out. Granted,
marketing in advance of a new service or product can help to
build excitement. When that is done, however, there needs
to be a clear launch date. You must communicate in advance
when your product or service will be available. Here is the
tricky part: you must adhere to the date set. Delaying a launch
can lead to distrust among your potential audience, which
is the last thing you want when introducing something new.
If you are developing a new service or product, you are far
better off stating a date that you absolutely cannot miss and
releasing it early as "good news." You can always make something available earlier; just never be late and miss the date.

The company MoviePass stands as a clear warning about
what can happen when the timing is off. The premise was that
for $10 a month, customers could subscribe to see unlimited
movies. Unfortunately, the organization was not prepared to
make good on its offer. Within three months, subscriptions
went from twenty thousand to six hundred thousand. There
were massive delays in getting subscription cards out, and
customer service was poor. The idea received great interest
from customers, but the company did not make its service
available in a timely manner. MoviePass has now been re-
duced to a penny stock and delisted from the stock exchange.

Whether the company can be saved is a big question.

An organization that gets timing right is the Catholic Speakers Organization, a leading resource that represents hundreds of Catholic speakers. They are all about availability for Catholic event organizers, making sure their customers have the right speakers. For the speakers or musicians they represent, Catholic Speakers manages the details of schedules, requirements, fees, etc. Their entire business model is based on availability, matching speakers' availability with the needs of event planners. As Catholic Speakers has grown and added more talent to their roster, they are able to advertise and promote more, making them the leading resource for Catholic speakers and musicians.

Isaiah 6:8 speaks to the importance of being available, especially when we work in faith-based organizations. "And I heard the voice of the Lord saying, 'Whom shall I send, and who will go for us?' Then I said, 'Here am I! Send me.'" When we say, "Here I am, Lord," we are saying that we are available to him for his work. It starts with availability. You have said yes to the Lord, and you are doing a specific work for his kingdom. Now, you must say yes, that your service or product is available for your user, because nothing will happen if it is not available.

FOR REFLECTION

How available are you to those around you? How can you prevent your work from keeping you distanced from those who need you?

What are some best practices you've discovered to make your message and services available?

Truth 36

AWARENESS IS A CRITICAL MEASUREMENT

"Then the eyes of both were opened, and they knew
that they were naked; and they sewed fig leaves
together and made themselves aprons."
— GENESIS 3:7

Awareness is a very critical topic in marketing. It describes a person's knowledge of your brand, service, and product. Awareness is individual. Different people have different levels of awareness of different items or brands. Awareness occurs, as indicated by Genesis, when the eyes are open and you know.

In the marketing arena, there are different levels of awareness, which can be measured by market research. There is aided awareness, where you simply ask whether someone knows of certain brands (Ford, Audi, or Chrysler, for example). There is unaided awareness, where you ask people which car brands they know, and they provide answers without any prompting. There is top-of-mind awareness, which is the first answer provided in an unaided setting. This is the first brand the user thinks of, and it indicates the highest level of awareness.

In the purchase decision model of a ladder (described in Truth 35), the second rung of the ladder is awareness. If your product or service is available (the first rung of the ladder), but nobody knows about it, then no one can ever buy it or use it. Having it available is critical and foundational, but your users must be aware of it to know that they can purchase or use it.

Awareness, therefore, is a key objective for many marketing efforts. Understanding who your customer is helps you develop awareness among those who are most apt to use and support your work. Obviously, having great awareness with a group of consumers who would never use your product or service will be of no benefit to you.

With your target audience in mind, you can create awareness through a variety of vehicles. Advertising is a common strategy for creating awareness. Social media also helps to develop awareness among your target audience. Public relations efforts can be highly beneficial as well, as they result in a third party conveying the information about your brand. It is important to keep in mind that awareness is not a one-and-done initiative. People need to encounter your brand multiple times before it starts to enter their consciousness. With repeated exposure, they remember it.

It's also important to keep in mind that different people take in information differently. What one person hears and understands may not be clearly heard and understood by another. All the more reason to repeat marketing messages frequently and diversify your medium, so that your brand becomes well understood by many people.

The Catholic organization Life Teen is an energetic, joyful movement bringing teenagers and their families closer to Christ and the Church. It is a wonderfully dynamic program that connects teens more deeply with their home parish through regular group meetings and powerful Eucharistic encounters. In support of this, they also host numerous conferences, retreats, summer camps, events, and digital evangelization. Life Teen does a good job of building awareness, because they clearly understand who they are trying to reach.

As you consider your organization, you need to know whether your members, users, and consumers are aware of you and guide them to understand your offering. You don't have to help everyone be aware — just those who could benefit from what you have to offer. Model yourself after Life Teen and help those who need to be aware of you and what you do. That is a second critical step in marketing and will help you bring people closer to you and, ultimately, closer to God.

FOR REFLECTION

How can you increase awareness in the minds of those who can benefit from what you offer?

How can you measure levels of awareness when it comes to your message or services?

Truth 37

THERE IS NO PURCHASE WITHOUT TRIAL

"I will keep thy law continually, for ever and ever."
— PSALM 119:44

Recall the purchase decision model of the ladder: the first rung is availability; the second rung is awareness; and the next critical rung is trial. Even with all the awareness in the world and broad availability, if the consumer does not "try" you, they can never become loyal to you. But trying once is not enough; they must repeat, trying you again and again.

Trial is when a user actually takes action; for example, after your parish is available, and an individual becomes aware of you, they take the bold step of walking in the door for Sunday Mass. That is trial, and it sets the stage for the future. During trial, the user is now considering his or her experience in the context of your brand, what you say you are, and what you promise. If your brand promises to be warm, inviting, and friendly to all, then when they try you, they are looking to experience that. If everyone is standoffish, they will feel as if your promise to them was broken.

It is critical that a user's experience be consistent with what you promise (as discussed in Truth 6). If their experience is consistent with your promise, then they will repeat. In the case of a parish, they will return to your parish Sunday after Sunday. If their experience is inconsistent with your promise, perhaps they will give you one more try, but you won't get many opportunities to fulfill your promise.

There are deep studies on consumer behavior that show how people make decisions. Consumers living in the moment don't necessarily understand their own decision-making steps at first. But people do understand what they're doing with trial. They know when they are trying something new, and they know when it lives up to expectations and when it does not. Trial sets the stage for their thoughtful engagement with your brand. Trial brings your brand, organization, or ministry to your user's consciousness.

Legatus is a Catholic organization for business leaders and their spouses. The intention is to help leaders deepen their faith while learning how to bring their Catholic faith and values to bear on their work as company leaders. Legatus has chapters all around the United States and the world, and it is making a profound difference with Catholic leaders. Legatus is an interesting example of trial and repeat. The organization is available in many places, and awareness is steadily growing among Catholic business leaders. However, it is in attending an initial event, trying the organization, that users develop deep understanding and commitment to it. Experiencing a meeting with Mass, fellowship, faith discussion, a keynote speaker, prayer, and networking is the best way to understand what the organization is all about. Not surprisingly, many people ultimately join Legatus after attending a meeting.

Often we dismiss the importance of trial and repeat, thinking that once we have built awareness, the hard part is over. Yet awareness without trial will never get you loyal users or followers. One helpful way to encourage trial and repeat is through promotional programs. Promotional programs can take many different forms, but they are all designed to get a customer to "try." A discount on a first purchase, a coupon, a loyalty card that gets punched when used, a free item with a purchase — all these are examples of promotions designed to get users to try. Often for parishes and ministries, encouraging current participants to bring a friend is the best means to stimulate trial. When that occurs, it is critical that you know that someone new is trying out your brand, so you can ensure the promise of the brand is honored.

For faith-based organizations, trial and repeat is even more important. You don't just want return customers; you recognize that souls are on the line. Yes, you want people to try your parish, ministry, or apostolate. But we know that your work to bring people to God is not "one and done." People need to return again and again and again as they turn to God.

You are trying to help people live God's law "for ever and ever," as said in Psalm 119. Ensure that those you serve can easily try you and come back for more. It is in the trying and the repeating that you are best able to bring them closer to God.

For Reflection

How can you attract new people to your organization?

In a parish, what are some ways to increase attendance and attract new members?

Truth 38

MOMENTS MATTER

"A word fitly spoken is like apples
of gold in a setting of silver."
— PROVERBS 25:11

Social media has grown significantly over the past several years and plays a strong role in marketing and communication. A clear benefit of social media is that it happens in the moment, in real time, and it brings your users, members, and consumers into the moment with you.

Social media can be used for a variety of marketing and communication tactics, and it is quite inexpensive. A platform such as Twitter allows you to engage in conversation with potential users or members. Twitter is nonstop communication and affords you the ability to convey your messages quickly. A primary use of Twitter for a faith-based organization is to put your message (which is the message of the Gospel) in the context of daily, worldly issues. This use of Twitter tends to drive awareness of you and your mission, especially if you are able to consistently engage on topics that are central to your mission.

Jen Fulwiler, a well-known Catholic author and radio show host, is very active on Twitter. If you are not familiar with her, she was a lifelong atheist before converting to Catholicism. She has since written books about her conversion, and she is a sought-after speaker on faith. She uses her Twitter platform to connect the dots of how she went from being an atheist to being a Catholic. Twitter is a great environment in which she can have conversations with others about converting from atheism to Catholicism. These conversations take place in the moment.

If you want to drive trial, Facebook might be a better platform for you. This platform allows for deeper conversation and messaging, while remaining in the moment. Facebook allows you to share more of your mission or ministry. You can set up groups so that people who are like-minded can join you in the discussion. There are ways to sell products directly through Facebook, if you desire. You can easily encourage people to come to an event you are having at your parish. Facebook is very community-oriented, so your goal with Facebook is to create an engaged community on the topics that matter to you.

A fascinating Facebook group example is Pink Sisters in Christ. This is a faith-based Facebook group for women who have had or are facing breast cancer. Within this very specific group, women turn to each other with questions about side effects from cancer treatments, for example. Importantly, everyone in the group supports one another in prayer every step of the way, from diagnosis to remission. Another example is the Catholic Working Mothers Facebook group, which brings together Catholic moms who hold jobs outside the home.

Instagram is another popular social media platform, and

it is helpful for building awareness through great visuals, especially photography. Organizations use Instagram to post photos of what is happening within the organization. For faith-based groups, this could include pictures of the parish picnic or prayer shawl ministry, for example. Instagram relies on images, as any messaging is shared using photos.

It is often wise to use a variety of social media, in part because the various social media platforms do different things and reach different audiences. Regardless of the platform you choose, the critical advantage of social media is being in the moment. Therefore, if you are unable to keep up with a variety of platforms, choose one and do it well and consistently. Others will take notice of you when you are in the moment with them, and they can connect with you. Your words, "fitly spoken" as said in Proverbs, will be like "apples of gold" that draw people to you and your brand. That is the power of social media. Moments truly matter, and you can use them to get your message out.

FOR REFLECTION

What social media platforms do you use to spread your message?

Which ones have you found to be the most effective? Why?

Truth 39

IT IS THE "SMALL STUFF" THAT MAKES THE BIGGEST DIFFERENCE

"A workman who is a drunkard will
not become rich; he who despises
small things will fail little by little."
— SIRACH 19:1

Surely you have heard the phrase, "Don't sweat the small stuff." This may be true in many aspects of life, but not in marketing. For you see, in marketing, it is all about the small stuff. Sirach puts it bluntly: "he who despises small things will fail little by little." There is great wisdom in this for us as communicators and marketers.

The "small stuff" in marketing refers to marketing tactics. Marketing tactics are the details of the implementation of your strategy and ensure that your objectives are met.

Each objective you set typically has several broader strategies that must be accomplished. The strategies then point toward particular tactics that you must use. By way of example, if your objective is to increase awareness among your target audience, then your strategy might be to implement Facebook advertising to reach your intended community. The tactics are then the exact schedule of the advertising, when you will post, how frequently you will post, and with what message. If the tactics are not implemented correctly, you will not achieve your objective.

There are broad categories of "small stuff" that should always be considered. These include:

1. The creative to be used: having a consistent look and feel will help your users recognize you.
2. The messaging provided: consistent messaging will remind your users what your promise is and why you can be trusted to deliver it.
3. The timing: users are bombarded with messaging, so being structured with your timing will ensure they see and pay attention to your messages.
4. Your budget: there are costs to many of your activities. Some costs are large, such as purchasing advertising, while others are smaller, such as making copies of event fliers. However, in all cases, you want to identify a budget and stay within that budget for your organization.

While these four things may seem small, marketing only works when the small stuff is sweated and done correctly.

Different types of marketing vehicles will also require different tactics. Awareness advertising requires great creative, understanding of appropriate timing, and a good budget. Promotions, on the other hand, have a "call to action," inviting your user to take some sort of action. This might be purchasing a product, attending an event, etc. For PR, a well-written press release that is timed with the introduction or announcement of something new is a critical tactic. Events require a different set of elements: the look of the room, how tickets will be distributed, what type of food or drink will be served, a program for the event, etc.

All of these various tactics are put together into a marketing plan. A marketing plan will help you identify the timing, costs, creative, and messaging to be used to achieve your stated objectives. Corporate America spends a great deal of time and money crafting marketing plans, and it is important for faith-based organizations to take this seriously as well.

To see marketing plans and tactics in action, consider brands that have multilayered efforts. IKEA is a well-known brand that provides affordable home furnishings, allowing shoppers to creatively design their lives and environments. IKEA brings this message to all parts of their marketing, from the store layout to their advertising. Even their catalog highlights their sleek lines and the shopper's ability to creatively design a space. Every element of IKEA's marketing works together to tell the story. The tactics — the "small stuff" — are executed with precision so that the overall story of IKEA is clear to all who shop there.

The Knights of Columbus are a well-known fraternal order of Catholics committed to serving their communities. The organization is international in scope, but the bulk of their work is done at a local, grassroots level in parishes. By focusing on the details, they have become well known all over the world for the work they do. Most people are familiar with the Knights at their particular parish. As they complete projects or raise funding for community needs, they are doing work that is specific to their community. They are a good model for "sweating the small stuff," because when taken together, they are well-recognized for the good they do the world over.

When it comes to marketing tactics, the smallest things are incredibly important. Do not fail "little by little," as Sirach suggests, by despising the small things. Instead, always sweat the small stuff in marketing, for this is what makes the difference and clearly gets your message of God out to those in need.

FOR REFLECTION

How have you approached areas of design, messaging, timing, and budget of your ministry or business?

Which of these do you find the most challenging? How can you change this?

Truth 40

IT IS ALL ABOUT CREATING LOYALTY

"Entreat me not to leave you or to return from following you; for where you go I will go, and where you lodge I will lodge; your people shall be my people, and your God my God."
— RUTH 1:16

The most important outcome of marketing is loyalty. For us, that means leading people to be loyal to God, as Ruth suggests. The entire intent of building a brand, communicating effectively, and delivering on your promises is to develop a relationship with your customer or consumer. As that relationship grows, your user becomes loyal to you, to what you stand for and what you provide them: a pathway to a meaningful relationship with God.

For marketing in the secular world, loyalty is paramount. Loyal customers no longer think through the options; they know what brands they prefer, and they are quick to choose them. When a consumer is loyal, they trust you as a brand, they believe your promise, and they know they can count on you to deliver each and every time. When a consumer is loyal, they also tell their friends, and they become an important part of your marketing approach.

Just consider the option of Coca-Cola or Pepsi. The cola wars exist precisely because the loyalty to one brand over another runs so deep. Those who are Coca-Cola lovers will never try Pepsi. Those who are Pepsi lovers would rather go without than drink a Coke. Encouraging someone to switch brands when they are deeply loyal can take years and years.

Another important aspect of brand building relates to what your parents used. If a mom always uses Tide, very likely her children will also use Tide. They trust it because their mother trusted it. Additionally, using something that Mom used takes a decision out of the process. With all the brands and advertising and logos to think about, relying on something the family trusted for years is an easy solution.

This is important to realize when it comes to faith-based entities. What parents do can and will influence what their children do. Additionally, recognize that it takes a long time to build loyalty. You need to deliver on your promise again and again so that people know your brand can be trusted. This is critical, because as people become loyal to your parish, ministry, or organization, you are paving their way to loyalty to God.

Consider Saint Peter. Peter was exceptionally loyal to Christ, consistently conveying his message. He was the rock upon which Jesus built his church, and he was loyal. This doesn't mean that Peter didn't have a few lapses — he did, and we know them well. But he always turned it around and reinforced Christ's message to everyone who would listen.

Or consider Mother Angelica and EWTN. Those who follow EWTN are exceptionally committed. Some people get all their news from EWTN. Importantly, their loyalty to EWTN leads to loyalty to God. They trust EWTN, so they turn to it for information; they learn about God's kingdom on earth; and this opens them up to God.

That is your work as well. You are creating a heritage for those to whom you minister each day. When you help people become loyal to God, you are assisting them to reach his kingdom, their heritage. Remember that your role in marketing your parish, ministry, or faith-based organization is critical, not so much because of your specific ministry, but because by drawing people to what you have to offer, you are actually marketing God and drawing people to him.

FOR REFLECTION

If you are a parent, what means do you employ to influence your children for God?

In your ministry, what are some ways that you can develop loyal followers?

Glossary

Associations

Elements that have a connection with your brand and give deeper meaning to your brand

Awareness

A consumer's knowledge of the existence of your brand. This is a critical first level of understanding as, without awareness as a starting point, there cannot be deeper knowledge of a brand.

Brand

The "promise" of an organization, service, or product. More than simply the logo or tagline, it comprehensively describes the offer.

Celebrity Endorser

A star who willingly uses his or her name and star power to give credence to and support a brand

Communication

The art of conveying and receiving information that is meaningful

Consumer

The actual user of the product or service being provided

Customer

The entity to which you directly sell your product or service. In some cases, this might be the same as the consumer, but not always. (For example, batteries are sold to the customer, Walmart. Walmart then sells those batteries to a consumer who uses the product.)

Demand

A consumer's interest in, request for, and/or need for a product or service. (This does not define sales, but provides an indication of the potential sales that a product or service might have.)

Evangelization

The work of inviting others to experience God and develop a deep faith by introducing them to parishes, ministries, and people of God

Logo

The creative mark used to distinguish an organization, service, or product

Loyalty

A consumer's commitment to a particular organization, service, product, or brand. Loyalty is a key metric for organizations as they try to build their brands.

Market Research

The technical work of understanding a marketplace, brand, target audience, awareness, loyalty, and other measures. It is typically accomplished through qualitative and/or quantitative analysis.

Marketing

The effort to convey a brand, promises, and messages in a way that motivates a customer or consumer to take action, consider, and purchase the product or service.

Medium

The vehicle used to carry messages forward. (Mediums can include TV advertising, social media, blogs, websites, radio, and many other things.)

Metrics

The key measurements that a brand uses to understand its performance, awareness, and preference in the marketplace

Offer

What an organization, service, or product provides to its participants or customers

Position (Positioning)

The role that a brand plays in a marketplace. Positioning is the work of defining that role with clarity.

Price

The physical amount a consumer pays to receive the service or product. The price should be representative of the value that a consumer will receive.

Tagline

A short, pithy statement that summarizes the promise of the organization, service, or product

Target Audience

The primary group of people with whom an organization, service, or product needs to communicate

Touchpoint

Every experience that a customer or consumer has with a brand. Examples include emails, brochures, customer service calls, sales calls, invoices, advertising, etc.

Trial

The first time a brand (product, service, or organization) is used

Value

The worth that a product or service has (typically conveyed in the pricing)

Acknowledgments

While God was certainly my coauthor, there are also many contributors to this book, and I so deeply appreciate each and every one of them. Deacon Tom Gottlieb, with a long, prominent career in sales and marketing for Anheuser-Busch, brought great depth and insight to this project. What a wonderful support he was every step of the way, considering Bible verses, editing, offering brand examples, and more. For his passion and support of this project, I am most grateful.

Jane and Leo Garvin — very dear and faith-filled friends, they kept encouraging me that the book was needed and enthusiastically share the book concept with everyone they know. Deanie Ries — a wonderful and deeply faith-filled friend, she jumped on the idea from the very beginning, asking questions that caused the book to be tighter and stronger than I could have imagined. Jane Tayon — such a dear, faith-filled friend and an amazing cheerleader to me. Calling every day, she would ask how much had been written and whether the manuscript was done yet. The many additional friends who encouraged me every step of the way, I thank you ever so much.

I especially thank Mary Ann Hutcherson, who heard about the book early on and offered great advice on its development. It was Mary Ann who suggested how to weave the Bible verses more thoroughly into the book. We lost Mary Ann to cancer in 2018, but not before she introduced me to many wonderful Catholic organizations, including my publisher, Our Sunday Visitor. Mary Ann's fingerprints are all over this book, and for that I am most grateful!

A very special thank you to my publisher, Our Sunday Visitor. Most especially, I thank Mary Beth Baker for her passion for the project and her insightful and careful editing of the work. To Claudia Volkman, who offered her thoughtful critiques to ensure the writing was on point. To Jill Adamson, who is so skilled at marketing and focused her energies on bringing the book to market effectively.

To my family, I am eternally grateful for your love and support.